I0101428

# Loving Life on Three Legs
## Tripawd Basics
## FOURTH EDITION

Canine Fitness and Conditioning for Happy
Healthy Tripawds

*Includes Coupon for Premium E-book!*

# BY RENE AGREDANO AND JIM NELSON

**LOVING LIFE ON THREE LEGS**
FOURTH EDITION: TRIPAWD BASICS
by Rene Agredano and Jim Nelson
A Tripawds Publication
https://tripawds.com

ISBN: 978-1-7334689-5-4

Published in the United States by:
**Agreda Communications**
240 Rainbow Dr., #14065
Livingston, TX 77399
https://agreda.com

Cover & Interior Design: Jim Nelson

DISCLAIMER: We (The Authors) are not veterinarians. All information provided herein is based only on our own experiences caring for our dogs Jerry and Wyatt, and the experiences of other Tripawds community members. This information is not a substitute for medical care by a qualified veterinary professional. Always seek the advice of a licensed veterinarian prior to making any medical decisions for your dog or undergoing any treatments or therapies, or if you have questions about your dog's health. We advise against any medical decisions made without the direct involvement of your veterinary team, and you should never delay treatment nor disregard medical advice based on something you read in this e-book or online at Tripawds.com. We do not guarantee that the information presented here will extend your dog's life, ensure a successful surgical procedure, or promote a complete recovery from amputation and cancer care. There is absolutely no assurance made of any outcome whatsoever. Neither safety nor efficacy is stated nor implied, directly or indirectly. Links to websites in this book reflect the content as of the publication date, and the authors are not responsible for any changes or unavailable content thereafter. Tripawds.com, is a project of Agreda Communications. René Agredano and Jim Nelson are not responsible or liable, directly or indirectly, for any form of damages whatsoever resulting from the use (or misuse) of information contained in or implied by the information available at Tripawds.com or within the pages of this document.

# About this Book

**Get More Help in Premium E-book.**

This is the **Basics Version** of our second Tripawds e-book, *Loving Life on Three Legs*. To reduce the price, content has been removed and the formatting optimized for paperback printing. Links to helpful videos, highlights from Tripawds member profiles, veterinarinarian quotes, clinical study excerpts, and more has been omitted.

For more comprehensive helpful information, photographs, videos, and bonus material, save **$5 OFF Three Legs and a Spare Premium E-book** with Coupon Code: BASIC5

❗ Save now at https://tri.pet/teb2

The true value of Tripawds e-books is the numerous direct links they contain to more helpful articles, videos, and podcast interviews.

NOTE: <u>Underlined text</u> throughout this book indicate active hyperlinks available in the premium e-book.

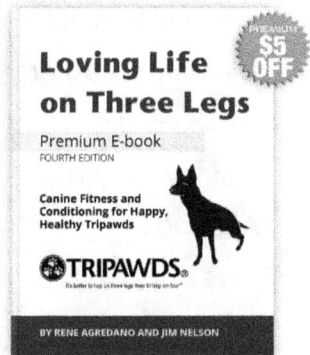

**Loving Life on Three Legs**
Premium E-book
FOURTH EDITION

Canine Fitness and
Conditioning for Happy,
Healthy Tripawds

**TRIPAWDS**

BY RENE AGREDANO AND JIM NELSON

## Save More on Tripawds E-book Library

Get two premium e-books in one! Download the Tripawds Library to save on both *Loving Life on Three Legs* and *Three Legs and a Spare* – our first canine amputation handbook filled with important preparation, recovery, and care tips.

❗ Get $10 OFF the Tripawds E-book Library with Code BASIC10 at https://tri.pet/teblib

# – CONTENTS –

# You Are Not Alone

## The Best Club Nobody Ever Wants To Join

Nobody ever expects their dog to lose a leg. If that happens, the Tripawds community makes the transition easier with education and emotional support. This handbook includes helpful tips for recovery and care. You will find **much more** help and support from many others who understand what you are going through in the Tripawds Blogs, popular Discussion Forums, Live Chat, and more at tripawds.com.

**!** For help finding the many Tripawds resources and assistance programs, start here:
https://tripawds.com/start

**Connect with Tripawds:**
- https://facebook.com/tripawds
- https://twitter.com/tripawds
- https://pinterest.com/tripawds
- https://instagram.com/tripawdscommunity
- https://linkedin.com/tripawds

**TRIPAWDS®**
**.com**

It's better to hop on three
legs than to limp on four.®

## Don't just take our word for it...

Leading veterinarians and 15,000+ members recommend Tripawds community resources and support when coping with amputation recovery and care for three-legged dogs.

## Veterinary Industry Praise:

*Tripawds is something you can check out, it's a community forum and you can learn and see that actually these dogs do really, really well on three legs...*

– DR. DEMIAN DRESSLER
THE DOG CANCER VET

*Tripawds...is a great community of three-legged pet owners... it's really a great resource where owners can share their experiences...*

– DR. SUE CANCER VET
WHAT TO KNOW ABOUT AMPUTATION

*Tripawds has a very important role to play – to educate people about amputation, to discuss options, to help patients with amputations...*

– DR. DENIS MARCELLIN-LITTLE
UC DAVIS SCHOOL OF VETERINARY MEDICINE

*If you and your dog are facing an amputation, or have just gone through one, you need to join Tripawds, the community website for three-legged dogs and cats.*

– MOLLY JACOBSON
THE DOG CANCER BLOG

*Tripawds is a place for people with three-legged pets – a community, a forum, advice about gear, nutrition... everything's there. I think it's phenomenal, a great resource that I send my [amputation] clients.*

– MICHAEL "DR. T" TOKIWA
THE COLLABORATIVE VET PODCAST

❗ Find more testimonials and podcast appearances with the authors on the <u>Tripawds Media</u> page. (https://tripawds.com/media)

## From Tripawds Members:

*Rene and Jim: First of all thank you for starting this much needed community. I do not know how I would of gotten through the last year without you.*
– BROWNIE1201

*"What a treasure trove of information and support you have created here! It's an excellent resource, I'm very glad to have found you all!*
– RH3ANON

*Thank you to everyone on this amazing site! It is so helpful to know that I have a place to go where people understand.*
– KKILLIONMEULLER

*The last 3 weeks have been a roller coaster and I couldn't have gotten through it without all of you.*
– JO & HORACE

*First of all, I absolutely love this site. It's helped tremendously with this new journey of continuing life with my pup as a Tripawd.*
– ROMYTHETRIPAWD

*I feel great comfort from reading all these messages, thank you for all the support. The more I read and the more videos I watch, the more settled I feel.*
– KATHRYN84

**Join the discussion at <u>https://tripawds.com/forums</u>**

Wyatt Ray loved life on three legs for 12 years thanks to proper rehab and his regular conditioning program.

# Introduction

Congratulations, you just made one of the best decisions that can help your three-legged dog. Whether you're thinking about adopting a three-legged canine, or your current four-legged family member is about to have a leg amputation, you've come to the right place for guidance. Gone are the days when the pet parents of a brand new Tripawd went home with instructions that went something like *"Tripawds can do anything! Just go let your dog be a dog!"* If someone just told you that outdated advice, we are especially glad you're here.

The truth is that while Tripawd dogs can do anything a four legger can do, it doesn't necessarily mean they *should*. Recent mobility studies on three-legged dogs and observations by orthopedic veterinarians tell us that over time there is a price to pay for losing one leg, regardless of the dog's fitness level, breed, or age. Over time, all Tripawds are at risk of painful conditions like early osteoarthritis and increased risk of injuries to their remaining limbs. If their human isn't good about monitoring their Tripawd's activity and diet, the risk is even greater. The good news is, there so much we can do to help our three-legged hero stay strong and injury-free.

As pet parents to Tripawds, it's our job to help our canine amputee strengthen, build stamina, stay safe and active with the *right* kinds of activity for their age, temperament, and breed type. This requires a little more knowledge and care than the typical four-legged dog. But if we are good about caring for them, our Tripawd can have an excellent quality of life, even as an old dog, should we be lucky enough to enjoy that time with them.

"He can do anything!" people often say about a Tripawd. You'll hear that a lot when you have a three-legged dog in your life. Most people love seeing what Tripawds can do, especially on social media. Scroll through Facebook, Instagram, and other platforms on any given day and you'll see dozens of inspiring videos of active amputee dogs running, jumping, and rocking canine sports. These posts are super inspirational and adorable, but the problem is that they only show a moment in time of that Tripawd's life. What we don't see is the long-term negative consequences this kind of activity has on a Tripawd, especially if they are not regularly conditioned with strengthening and

@tripawds

balance exercises. Many people don't know how important these activities are when it comes to keeping a Tripawd safe from injury.

Sadly, every day a Tripawd parent somewhere will see the consequences of inappropriate activity on their own dog. Which is why the Tripawds community exists. It's our mission to help folks through tough times, and not just when facing amputation for their dog. We want to help them avoid those injuries in the first place! All new Tripawd parents need know that it's our responsibility to monitor and modify our dog's activities in order to prevent mobility problems. It's even more important to do even if they appear to be getting around just fine.

Most Tripawds start out life on three with the ability to do walk, jump, and do other activities, just like their four-legged friends. But if that activity goes unchecked, they pay a big price for keeping up with the pack. To ensure a good quality-of-life, pet parents must keep their Tripawd's activity level in check, and ensure a healthy weight. We are here to help great pet parents like you learn how to do that, by sharing the latest evidence-based information about caring for amputee pets. If you're reading this book we suspect that's what you are looking for.

There's a lot to know about caring for a three-legged dog. We cover what you need to know in this book. Meanwhile, don't let your worries overwhelm you. Whether a dog is losing a leg to cancer, an accident, or was born with a limb difference, Tripawds can live great lives just like any other dog. You don't need an advanced degree to help your dog do that. But what you do need is a commitment to keep your dog at an ideal weight, and spending a few minutes each week doing prescribed exercises that strengthen muscles, treat and prevent pain, joint stress, and injuries. By committing to a relatively easy health routine, your three-legged hero can stay active and healthy for life.

## Is your dog a Tripawd yet?

If your current dog hasn't had a leg amputation and you're still weighing the pros and cons of surgery, check out our first book, <u>Three Legs & a Spare: The Canine Amputation Recovery and Care Handbook</u>. It's written for pet parents who just got the bad news that their dog needs to lose a leg. The book contains lots more pre-surgery and post-amputation recovery tips. It also features cancer therapy information to help you decide if amputation and follow-up treatment is right for your dog.

**!** Use Coupon Code BASIC5 for <u>$5 OFF Three legs and a Spare Premium E-book</u>.

## We Learned About Tripawd Care the Hard Way

Back in 2006 if you had told us we would be managing the largest community for animal amputees and their people, we would not have believed you. Back then, we didn't even know dogs got cancer! We found out the hard way, when our dog Jerry lost a leg to a bone cancer called "osteosarcoma." Even more shocking was learning that amputation would be the best way to help him quickly get rid of the pain, even if it didn't cure the cancer. The prognosis was tragic—vets gave him just six months to live. But we proceeded anyways because at 8 years young, we felt that Jerry had a lot of miles left in him.

Amputation for a dog is a big deal! In many people's eyes, a dog with one less leg is not having a good quality of life. We did too, at first. Then we watched a YouTube video featuring a three-legged Great Dane digging for gophers with one front paw. It boosted our confidence to think that our 75-pound dog might do just as well at that 150 pound giant. But we still felt so alone and scared of what the future held. So we started a little blog called "Tripawds" as a way to cope with our uncertainties, and also to share his progress with family and friends. We spelled it that way because after learning that veterinarians call three-legged dogs "tripods", we wanted to empower the word.

At the time we felt like were were the only pet parents out there coping with a situation like this. But quickly and mysteriously, Jerry's blog's readership grew! Other pet parents coping with their dog's amputation surgery found us. They started asking for tips about life on three legs, like "How will my dog go to the bathroom?" The only problem is that we were just two people with one German Shepherd who had a specific type of cancer. To encourage information sharing, we installed discussion forums to facilitate communication within the community. Then we added a live chat room, and further developed the Tripawds Blogs network to host free blogs for pet parents just like us.

We didn't know anything about Tripawd health and fitness at the time. On that unforgettable Thanksgiving Day we retrieved Jerry from the hospital and witnessed him taking his first steps on three legs, we had loads of questions for his surgeon. One of the first things we asked was, "How long until we can go on hikes again?" We didn't know that at the time, hardly anything was known about a Tripawd's physiological needs. Canine rehab was a brand new field. Our vet tried to make us feel good about amputating the bad leg, so he gave us vague answers as if to avoid getting our hopes up. "Take it slow and see how he does. But he probably won't be doing those long hikes again." We agreed, but secretly we hoped that Jerry would be different.

We knew that Jerry was our fit, strong, hiking buddy, so why wouldn't he be able to get back on the trail again? Unfortunately we had no idea about how much losing one leg would impact his strength, stamina, or balance. And since every dog's "new normal" is different, our vet didn't know either. It seemed logical to make Jerry take it easy during recovery, so that's what we did. We didn't let him walk more than a few minutes during that time, and carried him up and down the staircase in our home before we discovered the Ruffwear Web Master harness.

Slowly and gradually, we ventured further into our old evening walking route though the neighborhood. His vet couldn't tell us much about how to avoid injury to remaining legs. So thinking he only had a few months to live, we sometimes let him go wild. He played Frisbee when we shouldn't have, walked him too long when we all wanted to explore, or chased balls way too far. Today we cringe when we watch videos like this, and are almost to embarrassed to show it to you.

**!** Video links from the Tripawds Youtube Channel available in premium ebook. Use Coupon Code BASIC10 for $10 OFF the Tripawds Library.

Thinking he was smart enough to stop for a break when he needed one, we picked up on our old routine of taking a brisk walk every night after work. Little did we know that we were still allowing him to do too much. At the time, we also didn't know that dogs will do anything to keep up with the pack, even if it hurts. Then about three weeks after his surgery, we went on a walk and Jerry abruptly sat down on the sidewalk. He lay there panting, unable to go any further. We spent 24 hours a day with him. But we were clueless about his subtle hints that indicated something was very wrong.

## We didn't know what we didn't know.

Jerry eventually recovered from that long walk. His painful episode taught us that we had a lot to learn about what he could do, and should not do. Unfortunately canine rehabilitation therapy didn't exist, so we didn't have experts to guide us. All we knew was that we didn't want to repeat that scary episode again. Keeping him strong and healthy, without smothering him in bubble wrap was our number one goal. We didn't know what that could look like, but we were committed to his safety, breaking out of old habits that didn't benefit him, and rethinking our definition of "fun."

Despite the veterinarian's prognosis, Jerry thrived against all expectations, even without chemotherapy. We opted out of treatment because it was six hours to the nearest oncology clinic, and we felt the long travel commitment would detract from his quality of life. So we hoped for the best. To thank him for all his years of devoted services as the "Chief Fun Officer" of our business, we mapped out a plan to spend more time together. In 2007 we sold our house, nearly everything we owned, and our home-based business in Northern California. Six months after Jerry's amputation, we left town in a new RV to travel country and enjoy whatever time Jerry had left. It became the adventure of a lifetime!

## Jerry paid the price for our ignorance.

We traveled knowing that his time was limited. It was an endless celebration of his life and our time together. And while we thought were practicing better, safer activities by doing things like only playing on grass and throwing Frisbees low to the ground. Our enthusiasm to let him be a dog was silently doing more damage to his body. He loved chasing his favorite flying disc, and it was something we all enjoyed doing together. The only problem? All of his legs went up off the ground whenever he jumped for it. Eventually, that caught up to him. One of his rear legs gave out mid-flight. He fell to the ground and yelped.

Carrying him home was the most terrifying experience yet.

## "You want to stick needles where?"

Desperate for help, we <u>took Jerry to a veterinary acupuncturist</u> recommended by his oncologist. She suspected he had a partial cruciate tear, and thought it could be helped with the ancient practice of acupuncture. It sounded wu-wu but we would do anything to avoid surgery. Then with just one session, we could see the effect on Jerry. He let out a sigh of relief during the treatment, and after several more, he was walking without showing pain.

The progressive vet introduced us to a whole new way of helping animals feel better, and enlightened us about the benefits of rehabilitation therapy for all dogs, especially ones with three legs. During the rest of our two years on the road, we did our best to keep Jerry safe and happy. He still had a great life without all of that crazy activity! Our hero was a walking ambassador for life on three legs, happy to be wherever we were, and beat bone cancer against all odds for nearly two years. When the cancer reappeared in his lungs and took away his quality of life, we made the tough decision to set Jerry free under the big Montana sky on October 3, 2008.

We tell the whole story about our life on the road with Jerry and how he inspired us to create Tripawds community in our book, <u>Be More Dog: Learning to Live in the Now</u>.

## Along Came Wyatt Ray Dawg

Jerry changed the course of our life, and after he passed, it became our purpose to carry on his legacy. We committed to growing the Tripawds community, to make sure that no other pet parent of a three-legged dog would have to learn things the hard way like we did.

Nine months after Jerry passed, a Tripawds member introduced us to <u>Wyatt Ray Dawg</u>. He was an eight-month old German Shepherd puppy who lost a rear leg after being tethered and neglected in someone's backyard. Excited for attention or eager to escape, the chain wrapped and strangulated his right rear leg. Wyatt's owners eventually noticed and took him to a clinic. But when the vet told them the leg was beyond saving and needed to come off, their response was, "Then put him down, we don't want a three-legged German Shepherd." Thankfully, the vet knew better. He convinced the owners to surrender the handsome puppy, donated the amputation surgery, and handed Wyatt to a German Shepherd rescue.

A few days later, a Tripawds member who was fostering Wyatt reached out to us. "You need a new spokesdog," she said. Soon we fell in love with the eight-month old puppy, went to meet him in Oakland, and a few days later Wyatt joined our pack. Over the next 12 years, he provided our greatest education about caring for a three-legged dog. He was young, energetic, and ready for anything. Wyatt showed no signs of fatigue when we played hard – at least, we thought he wasn't showing signs. We weren't familiar with a <u>dog's pain signals</u> back then. Monitoring his activity was tough, and we didn't always stop him from doing crazy stunts. It was hard to know when we should allow him to "be a dog" and when we should reel him in. On our <u>Tripawds YouTube channel</u>, we shared videos of Wyatt running and playing, doing risky things long before we knew about preventing injuries in Tripawds. He was so energetic and unstoppable, it seemed like he would never slow down.

But over time, the more orthopedic veterinarians and rehabilitation experts we interviewed, the more they helped us understand that it was our obligation to work extra hard in order prevent arthritis in Wyatt's body. As Wyatt became an adult dog, we got better about following common sense mobility tips for all Tripawds such as,

▶ keeping his weight down
▶ making sure he got the *right* kind of exercise
▶ and providing good joint support

Despite our dedication to following expert recommendations, Wyatt's mobility began a gradual decline at age nine. As we reported in "<u>Wyatt's Time for Tripawd Rehab Therapy at Colorado State, Part 1</u>, in 2017 we started taking Wyatt to rehabilitation therapy sessions and orthopedic check-ins. As his stamina and strength decreased, he was diagnosed with hip dysplasia, muscle soreness and strain in his legs, shoulders and hips. His rehab therapy team prescribed Tripawd friendly exercises, and pain relievers. Wyatt's daily rehab program changed as his body did, and his stamina, strength and endurance stayed at a level that allowed him to enjoy a good quality of life. When he was ten, we got him a <u>wheelchair, too</u>. Eventually time caught up with our wild boy.

Wyatt developed tendinopathy, arthritis and bursitis in the tarsus joint of his remaining limb, and a worsening case of hip dysplasia. Muscle soreness and joint strain also took a toll. Sadly, Wyatt became too painful to enjoy life when suspected Intravertebral Disc Disease (IVDD) left him incontinent and immobile at age 12. It was 2020, and without the quality of life he once enjoyed, in November we had to set him free.

We know we did the best we could while raising Wyatt. The experience taught us that even <u>the most fit Tripawd experiences mobility problems</u>. His story and those of other long-time Tripawds we have known have since showed us that despite anyone's best efforts to keep a Tripawd healthy and strong, a three-legged gait still takes a serious toll on a dog's body. The good news is we can do plenty to minimize the damage. And if we don't, our Tripawd's pain issues will get much worse, much sooner, if the dog is not kept in good shape.

## And Now, Introducing Nellie: Our 3 1/2 Legged Spokesdog

In 2022, we adopted <u>Nellie B. Dawg</u> just 48 hours before she was going to be euthanized at a California animal shelter. Middle-aged, overweight, and with a malformed leg that affects her mobility, she had such a low chance of being adopted that shelter staff didn't even list her on Petfinder.

We started out as her foster parents, and eventually her foster failures. She's easy to love, with a sweet personality somewhere in-between Jerry's gentle demeanor and Wyatt's determined, devilish streak. She's a great traveling dog too, and happily accompanies us on our RV adventures. Her future as a 3.5-legged dog is uncertain as we write this. The malformed leg she lugs around is not directly causing pain, but it forces her to walk with such an odd gait that other joints are bearing the burden. Corrective surgery and a brace may or may not help so for now we are managing with strict weight control, pain management, and rehab therapy exercises prescribed by her vet team.

## What You Will Learn in this Book

You are reading the key to help your dog avoid the worst problems a Tripawd will likely experience over time. Now you don't have to learn things the hard way like we did, and like many people still do today. The information presented is a compilation of sixteen-plus years of interviews and discussions at Tripawds. You'll learn the best tips from professional canine rehabilitation therapists, veterinarians and others in the community who understand the physical needs of canine amputees. This book is a compilation of Tripawds articles that feature the most important things you need to know about life on three legs, including:

▶ How breed, size, and age affects a Tripawd
▶ Amputation surgery recovery and pain management.
▶ What a "new normal" looks like for you and your
   3-legged dog
▶ The benefits of canine rehabilitation therapy (and how
   to find a good team)
▶ Recognizing pain, managing injuries and knowing
   when to get help
▶ Diet, supplements, and nutrition tips
▶ And caring for a senior Tripawd

This book is filled with hundreds of direct links to specific Tripawds News blog posts, forum topics and videos. It's available in a print version, but we know you will find the e-book version to be much more helpful. It features links with direct access to information presented at Tripawds.com as well as other resources we've discovered. And just like we update Three Legs & a Spare every few years, when we publish new editions of this book, previous buyers can get a free updated version upon request.

The canine rehabilitation field breaks new ground every year. New therapies are always being presented and information is always evolving. We strive to present as much information as possible, but if you have more tips, recommendations and want to share your Tripawd's canine rehabilitation experience, please visit our Hopping Around Discussion Forum Topic. Tripawds wouldn't be the comprehensive resource that it is without the knowledge and sharing of members like you.

## Our Promise: Guilt-Free Reading

Remember that we are not veterinarians or rehab therapists. We are parents just like you who are looking for ways to keep our Tripawds healthy and strong throughout their lives. Tripawds brings members like you the most up-to-date information about fitness, health and nutrition for Tripawds. We do not advocate for one type of treatment or protocol over another, but we also encourage everyone to consider both "natural" integrative medicine and conventional treatments to help their Tripawd feel good. We have made very effort to contact the most highly skilled and knowledgeable members of the veterinary community, but we can't guarantee that your vet will agree with their opinions, or that these recommendations will prevent injury or heal any existing injuries your dog might have. Veterinary science is constantly evolving. What was true yesterday might not be tomorrow. What is in this book may be outdated before our next revision (usually about every 3 years).

When it comes to living life on three legs, know that there are no "right" or "wrong" choices, just well-educated ones. We promise not to make you feel guilty over Tripawd care recommendations that you aren't able to pursue. Everyone at Tripawds understands how amputation costs and follow up medical care can put a family in a financial hole. Not everyone lives near the type of specialty care than can make a difference. That's OK! Take what you will from this information and do what you can, but don't beat yourself up if you can't implement all of these suggestions. As a friend once told us, the best way to create positive changes in your world is to consider doing the least you can do . . . and then commit to doing at least that much.

Please share the information you learn here by talking to with your veterinary team about your dog's needs. Good Tripawd health is a team effort! With each little hop and pawsitive change that you can make, the life you share with your Tripawd will be as healthy and strong as possible.

Sincerely,

*Rene Agredano and Jim Nelson*

Founders, <u>Tripawds</u>
Authors, <u>Be More Dog</u>

## Need Help Navigating the Tripawds Community?

Tripawds is a network of more than 2000 three-legged dog and cat blogs. Members find the most help and support from others in the discussion forums. For help finding all our many resources and assistance programs, start here. Watch the Tripawds Tutorial Video for more help navigating the forums and blogs.

**Primary Tripawds Resources:**
- https://tripawds.com/start
- https://tripawds.com/forums
- https://gear.tripawds.com
- https://downloads.tripawds.com
- https://gifts.tripawds.com
- https://tripawds.org

CHAPTER 1
# The "Let Your Dog Be a Dog" Myth

Tripawds can technically do anything a four-legged dog can do. But just because they can, it doesn't mean they should. There are many reasons for this, which we discuss in these pages. But essentially veterinary experts now tell us that the outdated advice to let your dog go back to what they did before amputation surgery can do more bad than good. Today, we understand that loving a Tripawd means a commitment to monitoring for the right kind and quantity of activity, watching and treating mobility issues before an injury threatens a dog's quality of life.

## Why You Should Not Just "Let Your Dog Be a Dog"

When our Jerry lost his leg to cancer, nobody thought he would live another two years. His vet told us "Just go let him be a dog," and we did. Thinking he only had a few months to live, we allowed him to hike too far, catch Frisbees mid-air, and engage in high-impact, explosive and risky fun. These are all activities we would never do today with any three-legged dog, no matter their age or fitness level. If we had known the long-term impact of allowing any Tripawd to "be a dog," we would have made better choices in the ways we had fun together.

But the truth is, back then veterinarians didn't know much about the physical impact of amputation on a dog. Sadly, many vets still don't! So if anyone, including your veterinarian, gives you the same advice we got in 2006, it's safe to say that you are getting outdated information. In most cases it's not the vet's fault. Most just don't see many Tripawd dogs on a regular basis so their mobility needs aren't high on their radar. This is why we recommend that all new amputees evaluated by a rehabilitation therapist who sees more three-legged dogs than a typical veterinarian. More on that later.

Since we started Tripawds, anecdotal and evidence-based knowledge about mobility and Tripawds has grown. Pets are getting better medical care than ever. Because dogs are living longer on three legs, we are seeing how inappropriate activity causes mobility problems. Every day, somewhere a <u>Tripawd is having a remaining leg surgery</u>, or being forced to rest because of a muscle strain, spill on a slippery floor, or other overuse injury.

With all of the knowledge we now have at our disposal, there is a lot we can do to avoid these expensive and painful problems.

**We now know that:**

▶ The abnormal forces placed on an amputee dog's altered gait can raise the risk of injury.

▶ The spinal column on a Tripawd has extra forces placed on it that negatively impacts the musculoskeletal system.

▶ The extra wear-and-tear on a Tripawd's body predisposes them to osteoarthritis at an earlier age.

▶ Keeping a Tripawd's weight down does more to help mobility than joint supplements.

▶ Walking any dog only builds endurance. It does not build muscles, or strength.

▶ Daily strengthening activities and balance games prescribed by a rehabilitation therapist are one of the best ways to help a Tripawd get strong and stay fit.

Sadly, many people still don't get this information from their veterinarian. Social media is rampant with posts showing Tripawds engaging in high risk physical activity, giving everyone the impression that it's safe. As a result, many new Tripawd parents unknowingly put their dog's mobility in jeopardy. And we totally get it, because when Jerry lost his leg, we didn't know anything about safe activity either. Nobody told us we could hurt him by allowing him to "just be a dog." But after one bad episode when we had to carry him home after walking him too far, our gut told us that he could get hurt. So we tried to play it safer by throwing balls and Frisbees a bit lower, hiking shorter distances, helping him on stairs, and not allowing him to jump down from high places.

At the time nothing was better than watching Jerry do what he loved most in the world. Thinking that he didn't have long to live, our enthusiasm to let him get back to "normal" was putting his body in harm's way. We didn't know it at the time, but even jumping up to catch a Frisbee on grass was a risky activity. About one year later, he paid the price with a suspected partial tear of his cruciate ligament.

Many years later, after interviewing dozens of canine rehabilitation therapists and orthopedic veterinarians, we know that there is a fine line between allowing our Tripawds to do what they love, and keeping them safe from a total physical disaster. We totally understand how important it is to celebrate a three-legged dog's abilities, but we also know the harm that can happen when Tripawds participate in risky activity that will probably lead to devastating injuries and expensive surgeries. We see this happen all the time in our community, and this book is one way you can prevent it from happening to your dog.

## Even Fit Tripawds Can Be at Risk

There is one thing that all three-legged dogs have in common: eventually, all of them feel the effects of moving through the world on three legs. Over the years we have watched this happen as Tripawd dogs grow from three-legged puppies into their senior years. The risk is still there for dogs who received top-notch rehabilitation care their entire life, like our friend Spree. She was Tripawd Queen of Canine Health Resort in Fort Collins, Colorado, a medical boarding facility where her vet-tech mom Connie managed surgery recovery needs for dogs of all ages and sizes. Spree was born with many congenital issues that caused her to endure an amputation, and multiple remaining leg surgeries afterward, including a TPLO and a bi-lateral femoral head ostectomy (FHO) surgery on both hips.

At age eight, she fractured her remaining rear leg when the metal TPLO hardware caused the bone to turn necrotic. This remarkable girl recovered from each health challenge because of the diligence of her mom and canine rehabilitation therapy team. They left no stone unturned to help Spree be as healthy and strong as possible. During her lifetime, the health care she got was what we wish every Tripawd dog or cat could have during their life:

▶ Ongoing rehabilitation therapy
▶ The most current pain management therapies
▶ Evidence-based, vet-approved joint support supplements

▶ Plus weight control and appropriate exercise

Despite the top-notch care Spree received, osteoarthritis still ravaged her bones. When she died at the relatively young age of 10, her mom donated her skeleton to her veterinary team for research. She wanted them to know what arthritis does to an amputee dog's bones, so they could help minimize the effects on other Tripawds. "I want them to be used as a teaching tool," Connie told us. "Nobody really knows what this (osteoarthritis) looks like in a three-legged dog. Now they can."

When we saw see Spree's leg bones in person, we were speechless. It was shocking to see how osteoarthritis can create such painful bone abnormalities. All normal bones have a smooth surface, but Spree's did not.

Osteoarthritis is often the result of unmanaged weight, inappropriate activity, genetics, and of course, age. It's common, and it hurts. But we have many tools at our disposal to help minimize the damage. We will talk about those tools later on, but just know that by reading this book, your dog is already at an advantage.

## The Effects of Age, Breed, Weight, Missing Leg, and Arthritis

Even the most fit amputee dog will experience more physical challenges than their four-legged counterparts. But every dog has different physical and psychological aspects that impact how bad those challenges become. Age, breed, fitness level, health and whether or not a front or rear leg was removed will all factor into how a dog experiences life on three. And one of the other biggest influences is a pet parent's ability and willingness to manage their dog's activity and weight. This process doesn't have to be expensive or complicated, but in general the more time and effort a person puts into managing their dog's mobility needs, the better the result.

### How age impacts recovery and long-term quality of life

Right after surgery, it's not uncommon for a middle-age dog to get around better than a younger one who just had a leg removed. Over time, that older dog might do much better as a Tripawd. The reason is because dogs who lose a leg as a puppy lack fully developed motor skills that aid in coordination and balance. Without those skills, they often develop a more unusual gait and movements than a typical Tripawd, which puts their musculoskeletal system under more stress. Over time, it takes a huge toll as they age.

"I'm particularly worried about young puppies losing a leg because the excess weight carried by the other three legs tend to lead to problems in these legs," says Dr. Denis Marcellin-Little in our article "Let's Talk About Amputation and Pet Prosthetics." The orthopedic veterinarian and professor at the University of California at Davis tells us "If they have any joint problems it's going to greatly accelerate the progression of joint disease. So something like elbow dysplasia or hip dysplasia will be accelerated. They will have much more pain in their residual limb. Also, it will lead to stretching tissues during growth, maybe even deforming their bones, because the loads placed on these bones are going to be very asymmetric. Deformity of the bones can lead to problems in the adjacent joints. The shoulders in young amputees become very loose. We see a lot of shoulder problems, a lot of deformities of the femur and tibia, maybe the knee, all as a consequence of undergoing an amputation too early in life."

The canine rehabilitation expert Deanna Rogers from Northern Colorado agrees. She says that older dogs quickly get up to speed on three legs because they already have some knowledge of their bodies and movement patterns. Younger dogs tend to lack that experience. They are clumsier when learning how to get around with one less leg. But whether a dog is young or old, Rogers advises pet parents to be patient during recovery as you get to know your dog's "new normal." You will need time to learn what your Tripawd is capable of doing and modify your activities accordingly. "The performance of the pet varies depending upon the pet's other medical issues, temperament, conditioning, and comfort," says Rogers. "Give yourself time to learn about your pet, and don't have any expectations right off the bat. Just watch and learn."

If you have a young dog who *might* be facing amputation and your vet team is advising you to wait on surgery (while controlling any pain that may be present), try to be patient and wait as long as they recommend. "I think it's better to lose a leg not too early and not too late," says Marcellin-Little. "When it has to happen, losing a leg in the middle of life gives the opportunity to be healthy and dogs tend to adapt better. We have time to become stronger and lose weight and dogs can move around reasonably well."

## How Breed Type Affects Mobility

Forward-thinking veterinarians tell us that neither size, age, nor breed type should exclude a dog from being an amputation candidate, as long as a dog is otherwise healthy. But the effects of life on three can be very different depending on the dog's body structure. "How well your body is put together is kind of a unique thing," says Dr. Marcellin-Little. Breeds as different as Bulldogs and German Shepherds have different types of challenges on three legs. For instance, when a top-heavy, deep chested dog like a Rottweiler moves around, they place different forces on different areas of their body than a dog like a Corgi. "The consequences on that are not scientifically known, but they have to be discussed on an individual basis," he adds.

When it comes to giant breed dogs, they can do really well on three legs. We see dogs ranging from Saint Bernards to Great Danes having a high quality of life on three in our community. But sadly, these breeds are often the first to be excluded as amputation candidates by some veterinarians who probably haven't seen enough large Tripawds during their time in practice. But if you ask an orthopedic-focused veterinarian, or just visit the Tripawds Size and Age Matters Discussion Forum, you'll see that yes, giant breed dogs can be happy amputees. But if someone hasn't heard of dogs like Ophelia the Saint, or Nicholas the Newfie, even the most passionate dog lover dismisses amputation as an option, especially if their veterinarian isn't on-board. If a giant breed has cancer, it's also common for folks to fear that their big dog won't be able to recover in time to enjoy a good quality of life. But one thing we've seen here over the years is that even giants like Thurston the Saint do well after surgery.   Generally, giant breed dogs recover from surgery in similar ways to older dogs.

For example, big dogs:
- ▶ often take a week or two longer to recover than smaller or younger dogs
- ▶ may need more assistance during the first few weeks after surgery
- ▶ need more time to build stamina and strength.

As giant breed dog parents know, big dogs are naturally more laid-back, mellow and oftentimes couch potatoes. Amputation just amplifies that chill behavior, because they expend more energy and effort to propel their massive bodies forward. Recovery isn't always easy, and it won't look like a younger or smaller dog's experience, but they get there! And when they do, they are usually happy to be free of a painful leg, and their new mobility only slows them down a little more than before surgery.

## What About Overweight Tripawds?

There's no denying our pets are more overweight than ever. In the veterinary clinical handbook "Obesity in the Dog and Cat," by Martha G. Cline and Maryanne Murphy, we learn that over half of all domestic pet dogs are overweight. When amputation becomes necessary, that excess weight impact their mobility more than it does for dogs at an ideal weight.

In our "All About Arthritis in Amputee Dogs and Cats" article, orthopedic surgeon Dr. Kristin Kirkby-Shaw, founder of CARE: Canine Arthritis Resources and Education, says that weight is a major consideration before taking that bad leg.

So if your vet says your dog is overweight, the situation is not hopeless. Many Tripawd weight loss stories like Lady's have shown us that a dog who starts out as an overweight Tripawd can lose the pounds and enjoy a happy life on three. Remember, we control our pet's food, they don't have thumbs. Your pet can lose the weight with your help. Talk to your vet to create a plan to help your dog drop those extra pounds. Getting them there requires more work on your part to get them to their goal weight determined by your vet, but the results are always worth the effort.

## Who Does Better? Front or Rear Leg Tripawds?

Front and rear leg amputees face their own unique challenges. Having cared for both Jerry and Wyatt we have first hand experience coping with both. And, over the years we've spoken with many orthopedic surgeons and rehab experts about the subject. Therefore, we can answer one of the most common answers we receive: Who has it worse, front or rear leg amputees? The answer may be, both.

## Front Leg Amputation Considerations

When you consider that 60 percent of a dog's weight bearing is on the front legs, the reality is that front leg Tripawds have to work twice as hard as a four-legged dog just to move around. "Losing one front leg is like losing two back legs," says Dr. Marcellin-Little. "Having a single front leg makes the head and neck more involved in creating a bit of a pendulum, shifting weight back to the pelvic limb and residual front limb." As a consequence, their stance is shorter and gait is more altered than a rear-leg amputee. The good news is that since dogs carry 60 percent of their weight in the front, they are overall a bit stronger when starting out on three legs. Over time, they will experience different challenges than a rear leg amputee.

Front Leg Tripawd Challenges:
- ▶ Less endurance overall. Walks will be much shorter.
- ▶ Going into a sit position takes more time and effort.
- ▶ Holding onto objects such as toys and food is more challenging.
- ▶ Elbow hygromas (pressure sores) are common. Sitting puts extra force on the elbow of the remaining front limb.
- ▶ They tend to jump higher than they should because they still have rear legs.
- ▶ With one less leg carrying the same amount of weight on the front of their body, it's trickier to balance when going down stairs than to go up.
- ▶ Their shoulder and upper back works harder and has more abnormal forces placed on the area, which causes muscle strain and joint stiffness.
- ▶ Front leg Tripawds are more prone to elbow and shoulder osteoarthritis.

"For dogs who have front limb amputations, the most common injury we see with the front limb amputation is in the limb that's remaining, it's injuries to the wrist (carpus)," says Sasha A. Foster, MSPT, CCRT, from the Colorado State University James L. Voss Veterinary Teaching Hospital Orthopedic Medicine and Mobility team. In our Tripawds News article <u>How To Prevent Common Injuries in Tripawds</u>, Foster says that "The muscles on the back of the wrist have to bear more weight when you've removed one of the limbs. In dogs with four legs, they carry 60% of their body weight on their front limbs. They split it pretty much 30-30 each limb. But when you remove one of the legs, now one of the limbs has to carry the full 60% of the load. In order to do that, they simply need to be stronger."

The goal with a front-leg amputee is to prevent "carpal hyperextension injuries," explains Foster. This injury happens when the carpus gets loose, and stretches too much. The earlier you start strengthening exercises, the better. Foster says that two weeks after amputation, her Tripawds are already doing prescribed wrist-strengthening exercises. "For example, they would place their front paws up on a box. Then we'd have them do a dog push-up or lower their nose down to the box and then back up so their strengthening the muscles in their wrists."

Many people are quick to say that front-leg Tripawds have it harder, but both front and rear leggers each have their challenges. And as Foster demonstrates, there are many things we can do to decrease discomfort, strengthen, and help our three-legged dog live a happy, pain-free life.

## The Challenges of Losing a Rear Leg:

Spending two years with a front leg Tripawd taught us nothing about what life is like with a rear-leg one. Everyone seemed to say that rear-leggers have it easier, so we wanted to find out when we adopted rear leg amputee Wyatt. As a young eight month-old puppy, we thought everyone was right. He walked and ran faster than we imagined, and seemed to have as much energy and endurance as any four-legged puppy. Before we knew any better, we let him play longer and harder than we should have. Sure, his rear end would droop after long play sessions or hard activity like running at the dog park, but we didn't imagine we were doing any harm. We had a lot to learn! It took several years before the effects showed up as hind-end weakness, muscle strain, and eventually, severe osteoarthritis. If we could go back in time, we would have done things so differently for him too.

During our 12 years of living with Wyatt and interviewing canine rehab therapists along the way, here's what we learned about rear leg amputees.

▶ Ear scratching is harder! You'll see rear leggers trying to do an "air scratch" with their residual limb. Have a back scratch device ready to help!

▶ Dogs carry all of their propulsion power in the rear. As a result, losing one leg cuts that ability in half. Jumping and propelling forward takes more effort, and puts more stress on the remaining rear leg and low back.

▶ A dog missing a rear leg has more difficulty going up stairs.

▶ Rear leg amputees put more pressure on the lower back, causing muscle strain and joint stiffness.

► Rear leg Tripawds are more at risk of cranial cruciate injury.

► If they are diagnosed with a spinal or neurological condition like Degenerative Myleopathy (DM), Invertebral Disc Disease (IVDD), or hip dysplasia after losing a leg, the dog will face difficult challenges if the condition isn't managed.

For many dogs, losing a rear leg increases the odds of a hip injury. This is because they lose their four-legged ability to kick both back legs out behind them when they walk. Instead, they must keep their remaining back leg underneath their body for balance. Over time, the muscles in their hips get tight, and hip muscle and low back muscle strain happens. Learning safe, guided exercises from a rehab therapist shortly after amputation surgery can minimize the risk. "For example, having them place their front feet up on a high surface so their front feet up on a chair or stool so they are having to extend their hip. This opens the muscles in the front of the hip while they are strengthening their gluteal muscles. It helps prevent hip and low back problems in hind limb amputees," Foster explains.

As you can see, both front and rear leg Tripawds have their own set of challenges to overcome. "No matter if you have a front limb or a hind limb amputee, the spine always has to rotate to make up for the missing limb," says Foster. "The spine has to rotate repetitively, it's not designed to rotate like that. We'll often see muscle soreness, muscle tightness, arthritis of the joints of the spine, and all of those issues can also best be addressed by just keeping the dog in really great shape."

Whatever leg your Tripawd is missing, it's up to you to ensure your dog's well-being. Getting professional rehabilitation therapy guidance as soon as possible, learning the right kind and amount of exercise, sticking to a weight management plan, and practicing common sense go a long way to help any Tripawd.

## How Osteoarthritis Impacts Amputee Dogs

Biomechanics (the way a body moves) change after an animal loses a leg. Those changes result in abnormal forces that put extra stress on joints, predisposing an amputee dog to early arthritis. Minimizing and managing that risk can help the dog enjoy a long, healthy and mobile life. But can a dog who already has arthritis be a good candidate for amputation surgery? Many people instantly assume they cannot. But again, the chances of success depend on the individual dog.

Dr. Kristin Kirkby-Shaw says that the reason for the amputation often overrides a dog's arthritis diagnosis. "If we are considering an amputation because of osteosarcoma or something that is significantly painful and the purpose of the amputation is to relieve pain, that's a significant consideration. But if there's underlying arthritis and osteoarthritis . . . it really depends on which joint is affected and how well it's managed. For example, a dog with arthritis of the shoulder or even hip dysplasia or hip arthritis, we have a lot of things that we can do and usually a really successful outcome with managing those joints with arthritis. When it comes to the elbow, the wrist, the hock joint, those are a little bit tougher."

Whichever leg is being amputated, the leg opposite from it will bear the burden of additional weight after surgery. "Let's say a dog has really severe elbow arthritis and we are looking to do an amputation of the opposite front leg, there are a lot of considerations to be made there," says Kirkby-Shaw. "So if we are amputating because of an osteosarcoma and the dog is severely painful and barely using that leg to begin with, well, they are going to feel better by removing that source of pain with the amputation. But you are going to have to do *a lot* of things to keep that other elbow pain under control."

With or without arthritis, altered biomechanics put <u>Tripawds are at greater risk of osteoarthritis</u>. Minimizing and managing that risk is crucial for a pet to enjoy a long, healthy and mobile life. "We are particularly interested in slowing the progression of any problem that's already there, such as osteoarthritis in the knee or in the hip. And so, we are going to have to keep dogs lean. We are going to have to exercise regularly to keep them strong. Stay on top of it, if we think our dog has a problem. We should seek advice and get objective information as early as possible," says orthopedic veterinarian Dr. Denis Marcellin-Little.

## The Promise of Prosthetics

We've all seen the inspirational stories of animals using prosthetic legs. And if your dog is going to lose a leg, you might be wondering if a prosthetic is in your pet's future. If so, you should know that for a prosthetic to be successful, surgical planning must happen *before* the amputation. A surgeon must leave enough remaining limb in order for the prosthetic to attach to the body. Unfortunately in many cases, this just isn't an option. This is especially true when cancer is the reason behind the amputation and the whole leg must be taken to get rid of the tumor. But for a certain population of dogs who only need a partial leg amputation up to the elbow joint, a prosthetic leg can be a game changer.

## Is Your Dog a Prosthetic Candidate?

If an artificial leg is on your mind, here are some questions to consider and discuss with a vet who is experienced in prosthetics for animals.

Does your dog have enough residual limb on the amputated leg? In our article <u>FAQs About Artificial Limbs for Pets</u>, Dr. Denis Marcellin-Little says "The more limb they have, the more predictably successful a device will be. Anything above the knee and elbow makes it nearly impossible." Dogs who do have enough residual limb have far more options than dogs who do not. Rear leg Tripawds with a partial amputation have more options for prosthetics than front leg amputees. And dogs of either leg configuration without any remaining stump have no good options for success with any kind of true prosthetic.

We can't recall any rear leg amputees without a residual limb using a prosthetic. But dogs missing a front leg without a residual limb are often seen using something that is marketed as a prosthetic. Unfortunately at this time, no device allows that front-leg Tripawd to have natural movement in their artificial leg. A dog using one also cannot normally use stairs or lay down naturally.

"The challenge with a full limb amputation and a prosthetic is that there is no muscle to propel that leg, says Dr. Mandi Blackwelder, a veterinary rehabilitation therapist and owner of Healing Arts Animal Care in Portland, Oregon. in our Tripawd Talk interview "<u>Rehab Therapy Treatments for Tripawds</u> she says "The dog is having to lean and swing with their body to advance the limb. And then lean into it with their body, move the other legs and then stand and swing again. It is teaching the dog to do something completely foreign that is harder in their head than three legs. If they get it, their light bulb goes off and they're like, 'Oh! This is what my mom wants me to do,' then super, because that's easier on the rest of the body in terms of balance and things like that. But we also have to consider we're still not using a leg. We're still, you know, throwing our vertebra to the side in order to place weight upon it."

It's possible that with the rapid pace of 3D printing technology, we suspect that a true prosthetic for a front leg amputee will hit the marketplace soon, so you may want to hold off on getting one until then. Meanwhile, consult with a surgeon experienced in prosthetics prior to amputation if at all possible. And ask yourself these questions if you're considering one for your dog

**Does my dog have a good prognosis for a long, healthy life?** Typically it takes at least a month or more to train a dog to accept and use a prosthetic. This is a difficult question to ask, but if your dog lost a leg to cancer, is there enough projected time for your dog to successfully use the prosthetic? Of course all dogs are different, and yours will hopefully outlive that prognosis. But this is the hard reality of a cancer diagnosis, and it's a question worth asking, especially because of the cost (upwards of $2,000, plus rehab therapy training).

"Maybe your dog has a tumor and the chest also has a lot of tumors and the odds of survival are low," says Marcellin-Little. "Therefore, maybe it's not the wisest thing to invest all that time and money into something that might even not come to fruition because we won't be ready for surgery by the time their lungs will stop working or the heart."

**Is my dog easygoing?** Getting a prosthetic requires multiple visits to the clinic, both during the creation and fitting process and later for annual check-ins. It also requires lots of unfamiliar people handling their feet and paws during fittings and adjustments. Dogs who don't mind going to the vet and being handled are ideal candidates. Those who hate vet experiences are going to become more anxious during the process. They might connect their stress to the device and not want to use it later.

**Am I ready with a good attitude, training time, and money?** Dogs don't naturally start using a prosthetic. "When the leg is placed in a device, the dog generally considers the device a foreign thing. We tend to have to train these dogs," says Marcellin-Little. The process takes money, time and patience. A pet parent must be willing to take clear instruction from the vet team, be actively involved in upkeep, and always on the lookout for problems. Being an active participant and advocate during the process is also important. "A troubleshooting owner, that will pay attention to details, follow instructions and interact effectively with the medical team will help with the success also," says Dr. Marcellin-Little.

## First Steps for Succesful Prosthetic Use

Still ready to move forward with a prosthetic for your Tripawd? That's great! Now it's time to line up your team. "If you're thinking you want a prosthetic, you need to have your prosthetic maker involved in the decision about how the surgery should go," says Dr. Blackwelder. "You have to have the surgeon and the prosthetic maker talking to each other." But even the best team can't do what you will need to do to ensure success. "When I do a prosthetic with clients, I literally say, 'Expect this to be a pain in the ass.' I literally say that, 'and be really thrilled when it's not.'

"We all have that picture in our head of the dog running across the field in their prosthetic. Yay! Right? But the work that it takes to get there until that dog has that light bulb moment of, 'Oh, this works like my old leg. OK!' Because they don't have sensation through it. The difference between a human (amputee with a prosthetic) and a dog, is that the dog doesn't know that that's supposed to be a leg. When that light bulb goes off, they do very well. But some dogs, that light bulb never goes off. And it is a heavy duty training! So going back a little bit to the candidate thing, it's very much about the owner," Blackwelder explains.

## Rehabilitation Therapy: The One Thing ALL Tripawds Need

Whether your dog is missing a front or rear leg, wears a prosthetic or not, or is elderly, young, or overweight, all Tripawds can benefit from rehabilitation therapy. We are especially excited that it's becoming more widely available because for almost as long as there have been veterinarians, pet parents have been told that three-legged pets get around just fine without any extra health care. This is mostly true, but now we also know that all Tripawds eventually pay a physical price in some way, and some earlier than later. A good example is our Wyatt Ray's acute arthritis and bursitis situation. Or, when Frankie tore his cruciate ligament.

For some Tripawds, a dramatic mobility problem that could have been avoided with rehab therapy will end up being very expensive to treat. Sadly, sometimes the condition results in early euthanasia if treatment is not affordable for their human. But even without an acute injury, all Tripawds experience a gradual slow down related to age and limb loss. It's not a matter of IF they slow down, but when. Young or old, big or small, all amputee dogs lose the ability to tolerate their same level of activity as they enjoyed before surgery. "Things like their walk tolerance is going to be decreased, their ability to get on and off the bed or the sofa," explains rehabilitation therapist Dr. Amy Kramer in our <u>All About Rehab Therapy for Tripawds</u> interview. "They may still try because their brain doesn't tell them any differently...and that puts them at risk for injury."

Three-legged dogs who have rehabilitation therapy after amputation – or at any time in their life afterward – do better overall than dogs who do not. "The ones that don't get therapy are more at risk for muscle strains and sprains and injury," says Kramer. "I have a perfect example of a dog right now that had an amputation and didn't do any rehab. She went back to usual activity which was running around without any harness, without any assistance on her own. She tore her cruciate ligament in her remaining hind limb. Then she ended up coming to rehab because of that."

## The Benefits of Rehab Therapy

It doesn't matter when a dog lost a leg, or why. Rehab therapy isn't just helpful for post-amputation, or for older Tripawds and those with cancer. It does great things for all amputee animals at any time in their life. A rehabilitation therapist can help your Tripawd in many ways, such as:

▶ Pinpointing your dog's aches and pains, and treat them with effective therapies.
▶ Creating a fitness program that helps your dog enjoy better balance and improved stamina.
▶ Explaining and demonstrating appropriate activities to you that will keep your Tripawd safe and pain free.

With a rehab team on board, you have a point-person who knows your pet's history. They can help your pet feel better sooner when something goes wrong. Rehab therapy is not an all-or-nothing commitment, either. A good therapist understands clients' time and money constraints. If you are clear and up front with what you can and cannot do at home, or financially afford, a good therapist will create a workable, realistic plan with at-home Tripawd rehab exercises to keep your Tripawd as fit as possible. Can one rehab visit really help? Absolutely! "During that first visit, they learn so much about their pet and things they can do," says Dr. Kramer. Ultimately, rehab therapy saves you on vet bills too. A fit Tripawd is one who is less at risk of injuries that cost thousands of dollars to treat. It's a great deal all around.

❗ Please check out the Tripawds Foundation's <u>Maggie Moo Fund for Free Tripawd Rehab</u>. This program pays up to $200 USD for your first consultation with a credentialed therapist.

CHAPTER 2
# What to Expect When Loving a Tripawd

Most people don't expect to share their life with a Tripawd. Those who intentionally seek one out to adopt are a special breed, so thank you if you are one of these pet parents. The majority of people join this community unexpectedly, not prepared for the road ahead. That's why we exist. So whether you adopt a three-legged puppy or adult dog, or your pup loses a leg many years after you met, this chapter highlights important considerations for caring for a three-legged dog at any point in their lifetime.

You will learn important things like:
▶ What you need to know before you adopt a Tripawd.
▶ Ways to make your house "Tripawd-proofed."
▶ Quick post-surgery tips for new Tripawds.
▶ How to explain limb loss to kids.
▶ The best tips from veterinarians about life on three legs.

## A Tripawd Can Do Anything – Within Reason

There are two types of pet lovers in this world. Those who would never adopt a rescue Tripawd and those who are instantly smitten by the three-legged variety. If you're the second type of person and are thinking about adopting a Tripawd, we thank you! We love that a three-legger has won your heart. But before you bring your new hero home, keep reading for important facts you need to know. And if your current dog lost a leg for some reason, and you're not sure what they are are not capable of doing, keep reading too, we've got lots to share.

### Tripawds are not the best hiking or running buddies.

We like to say that Tripawds can do anything, but within reason. So if you are an active person who loves taking your dog everywhere, it's important to know that with rare exceptions, most amputee dogs do not make good running and hiking companions. Although younger dogs can often hike a few miles with their human, and may even be able to fly through the air catching balls or competing in explosive sports or agility, please remember what the world's best veterinarians have said over the years: all Tripawds, even the most fit ones, will eventually pay a hefty price for activity that pushes them past their physiological limitations. "So often, people only think of exercise as catching a Frisbee or retrieving a ball," says <u>Dr. Marcelin-Little</u>. "By human terms, that would be extremely violent exercise and they are not exercise that most people will do for themselves. But they tend to think of dogs for some reason very differently than they think of themselves."

### Shorter, more frequent walks are best for all Tripawds.

Multiple daily, short, walks instead of one or two long ones are the best way to reduce the risk of joint stress and injury. A Tripawd dog should only walk 10-20 minutes, two to three times a day. Anything more than that places unnecessary stress on their bodies.

### Tripawds will try to keep up with canine siblings, even if it hurts

If you have other animals in the house, you will need to pay extra attention to your Tripawd's physical needs. This is especially true if your other animals have all four legs. Animals don't like to show their weaknesses, and will do their best to keep running, chasing and romping with the others to avoid looking weak. When you love a Tripawd, it's your job to monitor walks and playtime so that the other animals don't drive your Tripawd into exhaustion every day. If this happens day in and day out, your pet may experience premature, painful joint damage and muscle strains that are hard to reverse. Starting slow and easy to gauge their capabilities is critical. "It's always easier to go up slowly than it is to repair the crash," says Dr. Blackwelder. "I mean it's hard especially (because) your dog wants to go. Most of these guys are like, 'I don't care. I got three legs. Let's just go! ' The owner wants to do something nice for their dog because they're feeling bad that they lost their leg. In those situations, I would say instead of going to the beach in that first month, buy your dog a dog toy and let them be digging around and getting treats out of the dog toy and things like that before we add too much because it is easy to overdo."

### Slippery floors and stairs are risky

If your home is not set-up for their needs, you'll need to make and live with some minor "Tripawd-proofing" modifications to minimize injury risk by keeping your dog's environment safe. These are easy and inexpensive things you would do for any senior dog, but you'll just do them sooner for a three-legged one. The biggest hazards in a Tripawd's home include:

**Slippery floors.** Uncarpeted floors are a Tripawd's worst enemy. They will try to walk on those slippery surfaces, but allowing them to do it isn't smart. Asking your special needs dog to walk on slippery floors is like asking them to ice skate all day, every day. It's something we would never do ourselves, but we don't usually think about it being the same for our dogs. The truth is, the muscle strength it requires to stay upright on slick floors is exhausting, and will eventually lead to a painful muscle strain or other injury. Covering slippery floors with traction is the kindest thing you can do for a three-legged, senior, or any special needs dog. You don't need wall-to-wall carpeting, but at minimum put down rubber-backed throw rugs, carpet runners and stair tread in places where your dog travels inside the house.

**Stairs.** Do you have a longer set of <u>stairs in your house</u>? Most Tripawds can handle going up or down a short set of stairs, say up to four depending on the height. But only if those stairs are carpeted or have some kind of traction tape on them are they truly safe. If you have stairs inside or out, consider how you will help your dog whenever they need to use them. Buy as many baby gates as your home requires to block off staircases. Also, if your pup is larger, you should always be there to assist your Tripawd with the help of a harness like the <u>Ruffwear Flagline</u>. A Tripawd should never be left alone to go up or down a long staircase on their own.

**!** TRACTION TIP: <u>Dr. Buzby's Toe Grips</u> are a nice addition for <u>traction needs</u>, but for total safety, no-slip rugs with traction throughout your house are the best bet. **See <u>https://tri.pet/toegrips</u>**

## Tripawds require more frequent vet visits.

If you are interested in adopting a Tripawd, you need to know that it will probably take more money, time and effort to minimize the risk of joint stress and orthopedic damage. Sure, we should do this for all pets, but this is especially true for Tripawds. We don't have hard figures to back it up, but based on our conversations with community members, the veterinary cost of a Tripawd dog tends to be higher than four-legged dogs, and we spend more at much earlier times in their life.

For example, Tripawds tend to visit the vet more often for orthopedic issues like osteoarthritis pain management. And certain breeds are predisposed to mobility issues than other breed types. For instance, large breed or deep chested dog breeds are more frequently impacted by the long-term effects of life on three legs.

The good news is you can do many things keep those vet care costs low, including:

▶ Maintaining your Tripawd's weight
▶ Monitoring activity levels
▶ Investing in rehabilitation therapy (or an <u>At-Home Tripawd Rehab</u> therapy program)
▶ Building relationships with the best veterinary care you can afford.

This is not to say that someone with limited income should not adopt a three-legged dog. But if you want to adopt a Tripawd, it pays to be mindful about activity and weight in order to reduce the costs of caring for that amputee animal. "Small decisions along the way with regards to activity and a way to make life a lot easier down the road regardless of the situation," says <u>Dr. Marcelin-Little</u>. "A small effort today will bear fruit over time."

## Quick Post Surgery Tips For New Tripawds and Their People

Are you bringing home your new amputee dog from the hospital? It's a lot like bringing home a newborn infant. You will feel uncertain and scared, but your dog parenting instincts will kick in before long. If your pet has just had surgery, here are a few short tips about what to expect when you pickup your Tripawd from the clinic.

### First, Adjust Your Attitude

As you start feeling the weight of your decision to proceed with amputation surgery, accept that there will likely be challenges over the next few weeks. You may be sad, or even regret that you went through with the surgery, but that's normal. Don't beat yourself up, remember to be strong, and know that the recovery time is just a temporary price to pay for less pain, better mobility, and more quality time together.

Go into recovery mode in a calm state of mind. It's a bittersweet feeling to know that your pet is alive and well, but that your dog's body is altered, and life together will be very different. Your fears are normal, but try to put those feelings aside for now. Celebrate that your Tripawd is in recovery mode! Sure, in the early post-op days your dog will look tired and a bit confused. But please don't mistake the behavior for <u>depression or anger</u> towards you. Remember your pet has had major surgery and is probably still dopey from pain medication. That is perfectly normal.

## Prepare for the Incision

The amputation incision is shocking. It's not easy to see your dog looking so vulnerable, wounded and different, but remember: dogs don't have body image issues. Your dog is just happy to see you and wants to go home to get well. So look your pup in the eye and not on the incision. Tell them that you are happy to be there, and excited for the future. This will be tough at first, but your positive attitude will set the tone for recovery.

## The Hoppy Tripawd

You'll notice that your pet's walk has changed to a faster pace that's more of a hop. Please don't feel sorry or think of your pet as now being "disabled" because they move differently. That unique gait is a sign that they are out of pain, feeling good and hoppy to be alive! Not long after coming home you'll see why vets call three-legged dogs a "tripod."

Front-leg Tripawds instinctively shift the weight of their remaining front limb into the middle of their chest, which is where the nickname "tripod" comes from. They tend to have a pogo-type hop. In order to propel themselves forward on one leg while keeping their balance, they need to throw their weight up into the air and land their front leg right in the middle of their torso.

Rear leg Tripawds also walk a little faster than usual, and have different stance and gait challenges depending on their body type. Tripawds with naturally angulated, low slung rear ends like German Shepherds tend to dip down even lower when walking, and may also take longer to build up core strength than other breeds with more table-like body structures.

## Recuperation Timelines Vary

All dogs are different in how they recuperate and how long the process takes. Recovery time is influenced by other health conditions, and we also see that dogs who have good pain management tend to have easier recoveries.

In our experience, amputation recovery generally lasts anywhere from three to six weeks. That doesn't mean your dog will be 100 percent back to their usual activities again, but they will be strong enough to enjoy short walks and quality play time. Some dogs have <u>tough recoveries</u>, but for the most part this is what we see.

## Hope for the Best, Prepare for the Worst

Animal behavior research shows that animals mirror our feelings. Keep a positive attitude. <u>Your attitude has the power</u> to make recovery easier! This period in your animal's life won't last forever. Dogs and cats do get their sparkle back. Not always at the same pace, but they get there. Focus on your pet's joy at seeing you and feeling good again. Amputation surgery recovery isn't a picnic, but it's not always hell either. You have a choice to respond to the situation with optimism or sadness. Be present, project strong, positive energy. We guarantee your Tripawd will feel empowered by your belief that everything will turn out OK. Even during the hardest recoveries, most dogs still handle the circumstances better than any human.

## Got Children? How to Explain Your Three-Legged Dog to Young Kids

New Tripawds members with children in the family often wonder how to explain dog amputation to kids. They are often unsure how kids cope with pet amputation. And they worry about breaking the bad news. Or how kids react when their best furry friend loses a leg. After all, even many adults have a hard time coping. But the truth is that kids and Tripawds handle pet amputation pretty well. It all depends on how we explain dog amputation to kids.

Young children and animals are more resilient than adults

imagine. Worried how your family's kids will handle the news that their beloved canine or feline friend needs or had an amputation? This story from Tripawd Griffn's mom Stacy will put you at ease. Her niece and nephew prove that little ones can bounce back as quickly as the pets. But it all starts with adults around them who set a pawsitive tone. Stacy shared the following heartwarming story about how she explained pet amputation to kids in her family.

**!** For member profiles and more forum discussions, use Coupon Code BASIC5 to get $5 OFF the Premium E-book. See https://tri.pet/teb2

## The Tripawds Recovery Shopping List

Wondering how to make your home safe for your three-legged buddy? Here's a short list of essential items that can make recovery and home life easier.

**No-slip rugs or yoga mats for traction.** Traction is a must to avoid falls and injuries. You don't have to cover entire floors, just enough to create a path for your Tripawd to navigate around your home.

**Canned food and irresistible treats.** Most recovering Tripawds have weak appetites, which is a common side effect of pain medication. Stock up on tasty food and follow these tips to get dog eating again.

**Low-sodium broth, Gatorade or other hydrating pet-safe beverages.** Spiking your pet's water dish with yummy flavors can encourage drinking liquids. Hydration is important for recovery.

**Fiber-rich foods.** Most recovering Tripawds become constipated right after surgery. This is a pain medication side effect. Have fiber-rich foods ready to encourage bowel movements. Pumpkin pulp, steamed squash, bran flakes and other similar fiber-rich foods can help move things along.

**Extra blankets, sheets and towels.** Sometimes a Tripawd will experience body fluid leakage at the incision site, usually diagnosed as a "seroma." The pink-to-clear colored drainage is typically harmless and part of the recovery process, but it can ben messy. Keep your pet's bed covered with towels. A warm compress applied a few times daily around the incision site helps to encourage fluid drainage. Most go away on their own but it's good to let your vet know this is happening. They may want to see a photo of the incision to ensure it's not getting infected.

**Potty pads.** Some Tripawds have elimination issues after surgery. Be prepared for accidents if your Tripawd is too tired to walk to their usual potty spot.

**Baby gates or other confinement method.** New Tripawds should be kept in smaller spaces to encourage rest and prevent excessive activity. Use whatever pet confinement method you can to prevent your dog from roaming around the home.

**Small T-shirts, boxer shorts, or baby diapers.** Placing the appropriately-sized clothing item on your Tripawd can discourage licking at the amputation incision. Bothering the incision can cause infection or pulled stitches and staples. The VetMedWear Recovery Suit is made just for Tripawds.

**Hot / cold compress.** Swelling and bruising after amputation surgery is normal and common. A hot or cold compress can help your pet feel better. These Heat and Ice Therapy Tips explain the correct way to use a hot and cold compress.

**Grocery bag sling.** Unless you have stairs in your home, there's no need to put a harness on your dog and potentially irritate the fresh wound. Instead, try this DIY Tripawd Dog Sling you can make with a canvas grocery bag.

**Tripawd-approved harness.** We love all the Tripawd dog harnesses in our Gear Shop for many reasons, such as helping dogs in and out of vehicles, up and down stairs and assist on slippery floors. The right sized harness for a Tripawd can prevent accidental escape during walks. But a harness can usually wait until stitches come out, since you don't want harness straps to bother the incision. If you have to use the harness, a t-shirt worn underneath is a good way to prevent direct contact with the straps.

**A recovery collar.** A few pet recovery collar alternatives are worth considering if your pet is known for outsmarting the cone of shame. But please don't go without a cone at all. It really is the best way to keep the sutures safe from itchy paws.

**Orthopedic pet bed.** Firm mattresses are best for Tripawd dogs or cats. Big fluffy beds can make it hard to get comfortable and possibly trip your new amputee. These orthopedic pet beds for Tripawd dogs get rave reviews. Introduce new beds slowly, because some dogs don't like the sudden switch to a new bed.

**Raised feeder station.** Animals eat standing up but when one leg is missing, it makes balancing while drinking and eating quite challenging. Raised feeders for dogs and cats help with better posture, stability, and digestion.

**Exterior ramps.** If you have stairs going outside, or a high clearance vehicle, ramps can be great. But not all dogs will use them. Most will not if they've never used a ramp before. We don't recommend buying or building a ramp until you know if your dog will accept using one. Dogs are born with poor depth-perception and cannot tell where the ground is located while standing on a ramp. Even with training, some dogs still find ramps too stressful.

**Pill Gun.** There are many ways to give a dog pills. The best way is to use a variety of methods and mix it up so your pet never knows how pills are being given. Having a "pill gun" on hand is very useful for when medication time becomes difficult. Greenies or Pill Paste have also proven helpful for picky pets. But use sparingly, since these treats are very calorie dense and can cause weight gain over time.

**Brain Games.** Get ready to help your dog recovery and keep boredom away with some fun and challenging brain games. They are far more exhausting than physical activity, bring you closer together, and can help your dog lose weight when incorporated into their daily feeding times. Keep the games simple during recovery, like these DIY recovery games anyone can do at home.

## Do All Tripawd Dogs Need a Harness?

The Tripawd-approved harnesses we carry are the best ones we have found to help a Tripawd navigate tricky floors, stairs, and vehicles. They will not technically help your dog walk, but they do help you help your dog in many situations.

We learned how useful the right harness can be when our front-leg amputee Jerry had to go up and down a tall flight of eighteen steep, rickety, steps to get in and out of our old house. And later on when we adopted Wyatt Ray, his <u>Web Master harness</u> came in handy for the same reasons. Today, our Nellie uses her <u>Flagline harness</u> nearly every day too, for similar reasons.

A Tripawd usually doesn't need a harness on a daily basis if they live in a house without stairs, don't travel much, and especially if the dog is otherwise healthy. But here are some situations when it pays off to have a Tripawd-approved harness handy.

## Three Reasons Why Your Tripawd Dog Needs a Harness

### Do you have a flight of stairs at home?

No Tripawd should be allowed to do uncarpeted, slick, and steep stairs without some help. The top handle on the <u>Ruffwear Web Master</u> and the <u>Flagline harness</u> are a huge help. This vintage video shows how we helped Jerry with his Web Master harness.

**!** All video links available in premium ebook. Use Coupon Code BASIC5 for <u>$5 OFF Premium E-book</u>. See <u>https://tri.pet/teb2</u>

### Is your Tripawd older?

During those first few weeks after amputation surgery, a Tripawd-approved harness can help you assist your senior dog with mobility challenges that are tougher to deal with during recovery. A great harness also comes in handy as a dog ages and grows weaker in their final months.

### Does your Tripawd travel with you?

Jumping out of vehicles is tricky for any dog, and it's potentially harmful for the three-legged ones. If your dog is your co-pilot, a Tripawd-approved harness helps your dog get in and out of your car, safely and easily. With a top handle to assist your dog entering and exiting vehicles, you have peace of mind knowing they won't put stressful impacts on their joints just to go for a car ride.

Tripawd harnesses are also a great tool for unexpected situations on the go. Say you visit a friend's house, and they have slippery floors. A harness helps you assist your dog getting into and out of the house. Or, if you go to the vet with your Tripawd and they need help on those shiny vet clinic floors. Our Tripawd-approved harnesses are great tools for that situation too!

## If your Tripawd is a homebody, you may not need to get a harness

From learning to walk on stairs, to going outside to potty, the harnesses we recommend are awesome tools. Some dogs benefit from wearing harnesses indefinitely. Others only need the help for a few weeks.

We know you have enough vet bills right now, and harnesses aren't inexpensive. If these situations don't apply to you, and your Tripawd stays home most of the time, chances are your Tripawd doesn't need a harness. Save your money for a nice orthopedic bed instead!

## Quick Recovery Tips from Veterinary Professionals

When we attended the Western Veterinary Conference, we asked members of the veterinary profession their best tips for new Tripawd parents. Here's what they want you to know:

- ▶ Believe your vet when they say animals do fine on three.
- ▶ Follow post-op instructions and medication dosages. Do not change anything until you talk to your veterinary team.
- ▶ Minimize activity during recuperation.
- ▶ Use extreme care on stairs during and after recovery.
- ▶ Make sure your pet gets enough pain control.
- ▶ Keep your vet informed about your animal's response to pain medication.
- ▶ Don't pamper your Tripawd too much but make her comfortable and safe.
- ▶ Get your Tripawd into a rehab therapy program with a certified practitioner.
- ▶ Consider laser therapy before and after amputation surgery.
- ▶ Keep your Tripawd lean and carefully manage weight to avoid problems.
- ▶ Have good traction and non-slip surfaces to avoid injuries.
- ▶ Preserve your Tripawds joints with quality joint supplements.

- ▶ Don't feel sorry for your dog.
- ▶ Practice patience. Remember that every day recovery gets better.
- ▶ Have a pawsitive attitude.
- ▶ Don't give up. They will get through it and YOU will get through it.
- ▶ Remember they'll recover and have a second chance at a pain-free life!

## How to Desensitize Your Tripawd's Incision Area

Have you ever noticed your cat or dog's muscles twitching near the incision site during recovery from amputation surgery? Or, have they ever jumped up with a sudden yelp weeks later? These are common signs of nerve pain, and phantom limb pain. Gabapentin and other pain medications are often prescribed to address this, but what exactly is "Nerve Pain" and how can Sensory Re-education help?

Ilaria Borghese is the creator of the TheraPaw orthopedic dog boot, and founder of Vital Vet – an amazing resource for all special needs pets. In our special Tripawd Talk Episode #124, Ilaria shares how to help our Tripawds through surgery recovery by desensitizing their body to nerve pain. This desensitization protocol can help rewire the brain after limb amputation, without additional medication. Ilaria walks us through "Sensory Re-education" with simple, practical steps you can take to aide in your pet's amputation recovery, and nerve pain management.

CHAPTER 3
# Mobility After Recovery

## How We Found Our New Normal (and You Will Too!)

When we picked Jerry up after his amputation surgery, we had loads of questions for his surgeon. One of the first things we asked was, "How long until we can go on hikes again?" Unfortunately he didn't have a definite answer. His vague advice to "take it slow" made it clear that he didn't want to get our hopes up, and he really couldn't say what Jerry's new life would be like. The surgeon simply warned us that Jerry wouldn't be walking as far as before, and to build up his walks slowly. We agreed, but secretly we hoped that Jerry would be different, that he would be able to get back on the trail and life could be the same again.

Jerry took it easy during recovery and we didn't let him walk more than a half-block for the first month. But as soon as he seemed strong enough, we allowed him to venture further into our old evening walking route though the neighborhood.

Then about three weeks after his surgery, we went on what we *thought* was a short walk. But less than halfway to our turnaround spot, Jerry sat down and would not keep moving. He simply couldn't. He was exhausted. That's when it occurred to us; we had pushed him too far! Jim went to get our truck so we could drive him home. And that was the moment we realized that our routine was going to be really different.

We were heartbroken, but we also saw that Jerry wasn't taking it as hard as we were. He was not looking back on the days when we climbed mountains together. He was not sad that he couldn't do it anymore. He was just happy to be alive, pain-free and with his pack! Once we saw how well he was handling the cards he was dealt, every day felt like a gift. Life became more precious as Jerry taught us how to stop looking back, and just stay grateful for every moment we were together. Even a short walk or just sitting in the sun together felt like a reason to celebrate. We gradually adjusted to the "New Normal."

Having a Tripawd in our life helped us slow down and appreciate all that we still had after amputation. Instead of taking our nightly brisk walk through the neighborhood, we played in the yard. We got to know neighbors who wanted to know why Jerry was missing a leg. The new routine showed us how Jerry's cancer battle could connect us with a world around us that we were always too busy to appreciate. Each day that he touched a person's soul with his sweet temperament and unusual gait, we were reminded to give thanks. We paid attention to all the little things in life that were now so precious, like watching sunrises and sunsets together, taking time to inhale the fragrance of freshly cut grass, and celebrating how far he had come since those painful days with a tumor growing in his leg. Jerry had been trying to show us how to appreciate these things many years before he lost his leg. But it took a lifetime for us to see it.

## What's the New Normal for a Tripawd?

One thing that took us a while to understand is that a dog is a dog, whether they have four legs or three. Dogs will do whatever it takes to keep up with their pack, even if it hurts. They will not tell us in our language that they feel sore after we took them walking too far. And they certainly won't stop playing with their best friend even if they have chronic pain that hurts.

Finding the new normal starts with an acceptance and understanding that life with our dog will be different, but no less fun or enjoyable. We know we are in the right place when we understand our dog's new physical limitations, find new routines that respect those limits, and do our best to continue giving our dogs the enriching activities they crave. This new normal looks very similar to all the things we would do to protect an older four-legged dog. You just do it sooner when you have a Tripawd!

### The New Normal for a Tripawd

You can start your journey to the new normal by thinking about what it means to have fun together. Tripawds can still have fulfilling lives, but minor home modifications, safe and monitored physical activity, and constantly watching for pain signals are all important things we need to do to ensure their quality of life remains high. Creating a Tripawd-proof, safe home environment is also one of the best things we can do for our three-legged dog. Here are some ways to get started:

## Take a look around your house and assess it for dangers.

Look for areas that could cause a physically-challenged dog to struggle or get hurt.

For example:

- ▶ Do you have slippery floors that cause your dog to "ice skate" when they miss the carpet and run around? If yes, get some no-slip carpet runners to place on their favorite paths. If your dog doesn't mind having their feet touched, <u>Dr. Buzby's Toe Grips</u> are a simple way to prevent injury from falls on slippery floors.
- ▶ Does your home have staircases inside or to go outside? If yes, do they have more than three stairs each? Most Tripawds can manage two or three steps as long as they are wide, carpeted, or have traction treads. Dogs may or may not use ramps because of their poor depth-perception which makes it tough for them to know where the ground is while standing on a ramp. Unless you've tested yours on a ramp, the easiest thing to do is put up baby gates to block access to staircases, even when your dog is recovered.
- ▶ Is your back or front yard sloped? Does your dog need to take a long walk to their favorite area? If yes, start training your dog to potty closer to home (especially during recovery). The shorter the walk on steep terrain while they heal, the better.
- ▶ Where does your dog sleep at night? If it's on your bed, a set of pet stairs can help them get up and down safely. Some <u>stair training</u> is usually required.
- ▶ Are your dog's bowls elevated? If not, get raised feeding bowls to help maintain proper posture and reduce neck strain when eating.

# The New Normal Outside the Home

## Managing Your Dog's Activity Level, Playing with Other Dogs, and Injury Prevention

Many people wonder what is safe and appropriate activity for a Tripawd dog. The answer depends on the age and fitness level of the dog, no two are exactly alike. It's another reason why we highly encourage people to book that canine rehabilitation therapist appointment for their Tripawd. A therapist is the best person to guide you on your dog's capabilities now, and in the future.

What we've seen in our community is that most active dogs can still manage a modified version of their favorite activities, like Farley, a nosework champion. Other less active dogs, like Jessee the Dane, kept on being adorable couch potatoes, only a little slower than before.

If there is one thing all Tripawds have in common it's that their stamina and strength will decrease immediately after surgery. It will take at least a few weeks before they start building it up again, but only if their person guides them methodically and safely. Those dogs born with a missing limb, or very young dogs who lose a leg usually don't have an "off switch" even during recovery. They will keep trying to do what they did as before until they collapse in exhaustion. Being extra vigilant about their activity level is so important.

### What is "safe" activity for a new Tripawd?

Certified canine rehab therapist Dr. Mandi Blackwelder provides excellent advice for activity dureing recovery on our Tripawd Talk Radio interview with her. "Even before stitches are out, if we're using a sling or a Help 'Em Up harness, something like that," she says, "I think those five-minute walks are great." She explains that, "the dog just had something serious happen but they need to get out and do their normal stuff. Smell the smells and go outside." After amputation, all dogs also need to figure out bathroom breaks. That requires adjustment once you've lost a limb. Dr. Mandi adds, "like how do I squat?" Even when missing a  front leg, it may take time to adjust. Mastering the bathroom break is a major part of being a three-legger. After surgery, returning to a routine where you go outside to smell the smells is really important.

Dr. Mandi offers great suggestions for ramping up that activity after surgery. She suggests, "If the dog had had 20 minutes [of activity] twice a day before, I would tell them to cut it in half. You know, do 10 minutes." Every dog is different. So she suggests seeing how it goes once you head out with your new Tripawd. Because they've had downtime during surgery recovery, dogs are burning additional calories and additional energy just in healing.

So, keep your Tripawd's activity level very low until you meet with a therapist for better guidance. Meanwhile, consider applying these guidelines to your own pup's daily routines:

▶ After stitches are out, keep walks to under 10 minutes long. Therapists tell us that shorter, but more frequent walks throughout the day are more beneficial than one or two long ones.

▶ Instead of jumping, ball chasing and frisbee tossing, play some fun interactive brain games like trick dog training and food puzzles. Tiring your dog's brain has a bigger calming effect than hard physical activity.

▶ Activities like canine nosework and trick training are fun ways to help your dog burn excess energy and stay safe.

▶ Soothing massages and gentle stretches (preferably prescribed by a canine rehabilitation therapist) can end the day on a nice note for both of you.

It might seem like a lot of extra work to have a Tripawd in your family, and we admit that sometimes it can be. But ask anyone who's ever loved a three-legged dog and they'll tell you that all the extra time and effort was worth it to have a happy, pain-free Tripawd.

## What about other pets & the dog park?

When a dog loses a leg, do other dogs care? We humans tend to worry about re-introducing our new Tripawd to other four-legged dogs and with good reasons.

It's normal to wonder about things like:
▶ Will other dogs attack my three-legged dog?
▶ Do four-legged dogs think Tripawds are weak?
▶ Can a Tripawd handle rough play at the dog park?

The truth is, most dogs don't give any indication they know that a Tripawd is different. Siblings might do a lot of sniffing when a Tripawd comes home from surgery, but that's likely because they carry vet clinic odors. A few people report that their Tripawd gets treated differently by other dogs long after surgery, but it's pretty rare. We think that it might be because the dogs are absorbing the Tripawd parent's nervous energy level when their Tripawd is around other dogs, but it's hard to say.

As for Tripawds who loved the dog park before amputation surgery, they will probably still love it when recovery is over. When Jerry lost his leg, we worried that he wouldn't be able to handle the dog park or day care. Wrestling with other dogs after his surgery made us nervous. But he showed he could handle the fun. Here's what we discovered on the road in Asheville, North Carolina, captured in this vintage video.

**!** All video links available in premium ebook. Use Coupon Code BASIC5 for $5 OFF Premium E-book. See https://tri.pet/teb2

Through the years, we've learned that Jerry wasn't the only Tripawd at the dog park who could hold his own with other dogs. One of the first times we realized Tripawds could do fine with other dogs was at our first big Colorado Tripawds party in 2009. That's when a group of Rocky Mountain three-leggers showed people at the dog park that Tripawds can have fun no matter how many legs the other dogs have. For more Tripawd parent interviews, check out another vintage video from the Tripawds Youtube channel.

Wyatt Ray also showed us he could handle things just fine, and would play too hard if we let him. In this vintage video, here he is running with a new friend at a dog park, long before we knew anything about better ways to keep him protected from joint injuries (please don't try this with your Tripawd!).

And check out our Tripawds Parties Forum for fun examples of Tripawds getting together. These get-togethers happen around the U.S., all it takes is one person to organize the fun through our Forums.

Throughout the years, a regular group of Tripawds members in the San Francisco Bay Area have held annual Tripawds gatherings to party with dogs of all leg configurations! They even made national news broadcasts at a 2023 gathering.

Then we saw how Arktik the three-legged Husky showed us that dogs with three legs are just as spunky as any at the dog park.

## Do's and Don'ts Tips for Tripawds at Dog Parks

Taking a Tripawd to the dog park is a happy day for many of us. It reminds us that our dog can enjoy living life and resume favorite activities. But keep in mind how much your dog's body has changed when they go from three legs to four. Before you head to your favorite dog park,  remember these tips for Tripawds at dog parks:

## DO wait to go to the dog park until your veterinarian gives the OK.

Ideally, you'll get activity clearance from your canine rehab therapist. Remember, your Tripawd has lost the ability to tolerate their same level of activity. "Things like their walk tolerance is going to be decreased, their ability to get on and off the bed or the sofa," says Dr. Amy Kramer, PT, DPT, CCRT, founder of Beach Animal Rehabilitation Center in Southern California. In this Tripawd Talk Radio Episode she explains. "They may still try, because their brain doesn't tell them any differently, and that puts them at risk for injury." If you must go to the dog park, keep your Tripawd on leash for some sniffing. Try to go during a quiet time when you'll have most of the park to yourself.

## DON'T let your Tripawd run wild without taking breaks.

Once your Tripawd is cleared for activity, remember that playing at the dog park is especially hard work for a Tripawd! Rehabilitation therapists tell us that the "explosive activity" most dogs love at parks, like chasing other dogs and running for a ball, are high risk activities for any pup but especially three-legged ones. The movements set up the perfect storm for muscle strains and even cruciate ligament tears. Most of us learn the hard way, as we did when we allowed our Wyatt Ray to go to dog parks when his body wasn't ready for that level of activity. We know it's a lot of fun to see your Tripawd doing what they used to do, but the hard truth is that dog parks are risky and should be a rare treat with plenty of supervision and break-times.

## DO watch for signs of over-exertion.

You can help your dog avoid potential injuries by keeping a close eye on them while they play. Watch your dog carefully for signs they are tired. The moment you see your pup sitting down, drinking tons of water, or falling over while walking, it's time to stop. Leash up when you see them look tired, and save what's left of their energy for the return trip home.

## DON'T make the dog park a weekends-only thing.

Dogs are most prone to injury when they become "weekend warriors." If your dog is a couch potato when you're at work and only running wild at the park on the weekends, they are at higher risk of injury to a remaining leg. Tripawds who go to dog parks should <u>always</u> be in top condition if they are going with the intention of playing with other dogs. Rehabilitation therapy is the best way to get them conditioned, and stay there.

If dog parks were part of your routine before amputation surgery, it's going to be very emotionally difficult to keep visits short, or not go at all if that's what your veterinary team advises. It's really tough for us to walk that line between allowing our Tripawd to just "be a dog"! After all, we chose amputation so that our dog could still enjoy life. But if we don't follow the advice of canine rehab therapists who overwhelming discourage explosive dog park activity for amputees, we are setting our hero up for a bad injury and more pain. This is the hard truth. But as Tripawd parents ourselves, we know that we will often over-estimate what our Tripawd is capable of doing, and feel horrible when our dog is limping or sore the next day. Over time, unregulated, explosive activity is an injury waiting to happen. So whether you are allowing your Tripawd to play at the dog park or wrestle in the back yard with a sibling, proceed slowly and carefully. Don't let your Tripawd get so tired they lay down and have trouble getting up. A little playtime goes a long way toward a healthy, strong dog.

## Remaining Leg Surgery: Every Tripawd Parent's Worst Fear

Most dogs who lose a spare fourth leg can adapt to being a Tripawd. But if one of their three remaining limbs is compromised from too much of the wrong kind of activity, that's when life gets hard for both the dog and the human. If you're reading this book, chances are that your dog hasn't suffered from a remaining leg injury yet. But the sad reality is many Tripawds will endure an orthopedic disorder at some point. We hear about remaining leg injuries all the time in our community. The evidence to support this predisposition is getting clearer all the time. According to one small sampling in this Tripawds Orthopedic Disorders Study, all Tripawds – both front and rear limb amputees – may have a susceptibility to future orthopedic conditions at an average of 1.75 years after amputation.

Common remaining limb surgeries for dogs include:
▶ Femoral Head Ostectomy (FHO)
▶ TPLO / TTA CCL Rupture Surgeries
▶ Total Hip Replacement (THR)

The good news is that if these or any other major leg repair is necessary, a Tripawd recovery from a remaining leg surgery isn't impossible. With the right board-certified orthopedic surgeon and top-notch rehabilitation therapy, most Tripawds of all ages can go on to regain better mobility. Is it easy? No. Can it take longer than expected? Absolutely. Is it expensive? Oh yeah. Agreeing to an orthopedic surgery for your Tripawd is scary for all those reasons. But as long as you choose a board-certified veterinary surgeon with orthopedic expertise at handling surgeries like this for a Tripawd, and have a great rehabilitation therapy team on your side, your Tripawd has as good a chance at a full recovery as any four-legged animal.

## The truth about remaining leg surgery recovery

Each day orthopedic experts expand the boundaries of surgery to help our animals live happier, better lives. As recently as ten years ago, most veterinary orthopedic surgeons would discourage pet parents from considering any kind of remaining leg surgery on a Tripawd. But through the years, more and more surgeons are finding that three-legged dogs can certainly make full recoveries from these procedures.

As our members have shown, it's not impossible for a Tripawd to recover from a remaining leg surgery, but it's no picnic either. If you find yourself in this situation, there are things you need to know about recovery and life afterward.

**1.** Don't rush into surgery until you get a second or even third opinion from another veterinarian at a different practice. We also recommend talking to a rehabilitation therapist for another perspective. Ideally, you'll find a veterinarian who is credentialed in both surgery and rehabilitation therapy. If you'd like help finding one, just let us know.

**2.** While you wait to decide, be sure your dog is receiving good pain management to cope with the injury.

**3.** If you choose surgery, you will need help with recovery. A partner who can stay at your home with you while your dog recovers is ideal.

**4.** Remaining leg surgery can be very expensive. Keep in mind there are other costs involved, like rehabilitation therapy. This is one reason why we are so fanatical about keeping your Tripawd's activity level safe, and their weight down. Both go a long way toward preventing orthopedic problems.

**5.** Your pet insurance probably won't cover the surgery or anything associated with it. It doesn't hurt to call your company for approval, but don't expect them to pay for treatment. As we discovered with our Wyatt Ray, orthopedic procedures are not covered by U.S. pet insurance companies at this time. Being an amputee is considered a pre-existing condition, and any medical needs that can be correlated with limb loss are also pre-existing.

The Tripawds News blog includes many blog articles about Tripawd recovery from remaining leg surgeries. Take a look and if you want to discuss your situation, be sure to start a new topic or search in the Hopping Around forum to lean on our community for support.

## Do Tripawds Cost More Money?

You might be wondering, does all of this extra care mean that a three-legged dog is more expensive in the long run? The truth is that it's hard to say, because the data doesn't exist. Also because veterinary costs depend on many factors, like where someone lives, how well they maintain their pet's overall health, and how much a person spends above and beyond normal veterinary costs. And then there's a person's perception of what "expensive" means. We all have different levels of financial ability to pay for veterinary care. But our honest opinion is based on our personal experience and what we have seen over the last 17+ years in the Tripawds community. If we had to answer this question, the short answer is: mostly, yes. Over the course of a lifetime, caring for a three-legged dog likely ends up costing more that a four-legged dog. Managing the mobility challenges and effects of life on three legs is just not something that most parents of four-legged dogs ever confront.

At the time Jerry lost his leg because of osteosarcoma, we had no idea dogs even got cancer! Afterward, we were much more conscientious about what he ate, how often he saw the vet, and making sure we tended to his aches and pains with acupuncture. His cost of care went up as a result. Later, Wyatt Ray would receive a higher level of veterinary care during his twelve years than Jerry ever got in his two years as a Tripawd. Today, our Nellie is really benefiting from the advances in veterinary care, so her cost of care is probably going to be higher than Wyatt's.

In our experience, the cost of caring for a Tripawd dog depends on the same factors that influence the cost of caring for any four-legged dog:

▶ The cost of veterinary care where you live
▶ The dog's breed type
▶ A dog's weight (overweight pets cost more to care for)
▶ How well a person manages their dog's activity level

However, when it comes to a three-legged dogs, it seems like Tripawds do tend to visit the vet more often, especially for injuries related to an altered gait, and managing the pain of osteoarthritis, a disease that Tripawds tend to experience at a younger age. But while we cannot control the costs of veterinary care in our area, we *can* do our best to mitigate the effects of three legs so that we avoid seeing the vet more often. By reading this book, you are taking a huge money-saving step!

## Care for bigger dog breeds costs more when they're three-legged.

Orthopedic veterinarians tell us that large or deep-chested dogs tend to be more impacted by the long-term effects of life on three legs. It simply takes more energy and effort to move around more weight. The altered movement causes larger breeds to suffer from osteoarthritis more often, and sooner, than smaller dogs. As a result, the cost of paying for osteoarthritis pain management happens much sooner than a pet parent with a smaller Tripawd. But all hope is not lost. Carefully managing a dog's activity and weight greatly influences the severity of osteoarthritis, and the painful costs to treat it.

## Too many extra pounds also influence costs of care.

Whether a pet has four legs or three, when a dog is overweight, quality of life goes down and the risk of many diseases goes up. These effects are even more severe in Tripawd dogs, such as:

▶ Excess weight reduces stamina and strength necessary to prevent injury during playtime.
▶ Moving around on three legs is harder than necessary.
▶ Being overweight predisposes dogs to osteoarthritis, cancer, and other expensive diseases.

All 3-legged dogs cost more money if their weight is not maintained. The good news is, Tripawd weight loss is entirely up to us. We will dive into facts about overweight Tripawds in our Diet and Nutrition chapter.

## Unchecked activity makes the cost of care go up.

Rehabilitation therapists tell us that yes, Tripawds can do anything a four legged pet can do, but should they? In most cases, no! That's because allowing your amputee dog to participate in unregulated activity alone or with other dogs is setting them up for an injury–and huge veterinary bills! If you are not careful about managing activity levels, prepare for a higher cost of care than other Tripawd parents.

## One Extra Step You Can Take: Choose an AAHA Clinic

The good news is that you can do many things to reduce the extra costs associated with three-legged dog parenting. Going beyond the bare minimum pet health obligations like annual wellness exams will minimize the odds your dog will require expensive vet care. Take time to build relationships with the best vet clinic you can afford. One way to ensure your pet is getting the best vet care is by taking your Tripawd to clinic accredited by the American Animal Hospital Association (AAHA). Here are two reasons why we feel that AAHA clinics are a great choice.

### Reason 1: AAHA Clinics Follow Tough Standards of Care

Human hospitals must pass rigorous standards by accrediting organizations in order to practice medicine. But accreditation is optional for veterinary clinics. AAHA is the only organization that accredits veterinary hospitals in the United States and Canada.

If a clinic is not AAHA-accredited, it doesn't mean they aren't doing a good job. Many non-AAHA clinics are awesome. But a big reason why Tripawds loves AAHA-accredited clinics is the peace of mind that accreditation brings. When you walk through an AAHA-accredited clinic's doors, you know that everyone on the team is following the same rigorous standards every other AAHA clinic follows. It's an above-average experience. Your Tripawd gets gold standard care, no matter which AAHA practice you choose.

## Reason 2: AAHA Vet Clinic Teams Commit to Learning

Every three years, an AAHA clinic must be re-inspected in order to keep their accreditation. Clinics need to pass 900 accreditation standards set by the AAHA organization. This means veterinary clinic team members must keep learning above and beyond the minimum continuing education credits required for veterinary professionals to keep their own licenses. From AAHA's latest Pain Management Guidelines to getting certified in AAHA's Animal Hospice & Palliative Care Certificate Program, the AAHA teams constantly strive to find new and better ways to help our fur kids.

Of course, there are many awesome vet clinics that are not AAHA-accredited. But their patient care protocols are not standardized or backed by a credentialing body. In other words, nobody but the clinic owner will guarantee that the vets at the practice follow the most modern veterinary protocols, or work at the highest levels of care in the industry.

The biggest drawback to choosing an AAHA clinic is that because they practice the latest innovations, and follow such strict protocols, the cost of care tends to be higher than clinics that are not AAHA-accredited. But we think choosing AAHA clinics means having an attitude of *"I'm paying more now so that I don't have to pay even more later on."*

These above-average veterinary teams at AAHA clinics practice the most current medicine not to charge you more money, but so they can get to the root of a health problem faster and help your Tripawd feel better sooner.

@tripawds

Unfortunately, AAHA-accredited clinics only comprise about 15% of all veterinary practices. AAHA clinics can be tough to find, since accreditation is optional and the majority of vet clinics opt out. If you just can't find an AAHA clinic near you, or just can't afford the higher cost of care at one, that's OK! Nobody at Tripawds will judge you for your choice. We just encourage you to do all you can to <u>learn how to advocate for your dog</u> at the vet so that you can still get the best care possible when you do need it.

❗ Check the <u>AAHA Hospital Locator</u> to find an accredited clinic near you: <u>https://www.aaha.org/your-pet/hospital-locator</u>

Loving and living with a Tripawd doesn't mean we have to roll them up in bubble-wrap. And it doesn't mean we will go broke either. As long as we are more mindful about their activity, weight, pain levels, and veterinary care, our Tripawd has just as good a chance at enjoying a long, healthy life as any four legger!

CHAPTER 4
# Understanding Proper Pain Management

## How to Decipher Pain in a Tripawd

We hear it all the time: New Tripawds community members often explain how their pet is "not in pain" even though they clearly notice the dog is limping. The sad truth is, *any* kind of limp is a sign that the animal is experiencing pain. Even if a pet is not vocalizing pain, is eating well, tail wagging, and seems otherwise fine, a limp suggests it is painful to bear weight on that leg.

Dogs are masters at hiding pain, and only occasionally give us a glimpse of their discomfort. They might want to go home sooner than usual on a walk, or get tired faster than usual after playing with other dogs. Maybe they walk with a slight limp, which we dismiss as "just getting old." And then the next day, they look fine! Sometimes though, those on-again, off-again clues are the ominous sign of something serious, like a cancerous bone tumor. That's exactly how we discovered our Jerry had osteosarcoma. The intermittent limp he had been trying to hide for several months was his way of telling us that he was hurting, but we didn't understand his language. Only after his limp was so consistent and obvious did we (and his vet) take extra steps to diagnose the problem. This resulted is us seeking a second opinion. Only then did we discover Jerry's painful limp was due due to osteosarcoma, the most painful bone tumor.

Unfortunately, this situation is all too common and we still see similar situations with many new Tripawds members. Learning how to understand the language of pain has always been left up to our veterinarians. Yet they often have difficulty distinguishing pain too! But the more science teaches us about pain signals in animals, the sooner we can pinpoint these signs, and treat the pain to help our animals feel better.

This cannot be over-stated: Animals will do everything possible to hide their pain. When they do reveal it, the signs aren't typically done with vocalization. They use body language, unlike humans who can vocalize their painful condition with words. A dog doesn't have to cry out loud, or stop eating, to tell us they hurt.

Dogs show pain in more subtle ways, including:
- Sitting down on walks or turning around early and heading home
- Reluctantly using stairs or getting up onto furniture, hesitating before taking a step.
- Slowly gets up from bed, looks stiff when moving
- Flinches when touched in a certain area, licks lips, turns to look at your hand
- Droopy or flat ears, droopy tail, scrunchy face
- Licking the same body part
- Not eager to interact with people
- Restless, unable to sleep

Sadly, many people also assume that because a dog is older, these signals are just part of aging. They are not. Dr. Ana Esquivel deals with this situation often. She suggests that "signs of slowing down" are often under-diagnosed arthritis that pet parents don't recognize that as pain.

By the time pain is severe enough for our dog to show they hurt, it's already at a level that no human would ever tolerate. As pet parents, especially *Tripawd* pet parents, it's our obligation to always be watching for pain. If we do not know the signs, and do not learn how to advocate for better pain management at the veterinary clinic, then amputation recovery and life as a Tripawd will be challenging, heartbreaking, and expensive to treat.

## Acute Pain Versus Chronic Pain

Physical pain in any species is classified into two categories: acute or chronic.

**Acute pain** is related to sudden trauma like a torn ligament, or an invasive surgery like amputation. The result is bruising, swelling, and difficulty moving around. Acute pain generally goes away when inflammation is eliminated and the body is healed. But if it isn't managed early on after injury, acute pain can turn into chronic pain, which is more complicated and expensive to treat.

**Chronic pain** is something that builds up gradually, and can last a lifetime. It's a common condition among dogs who have lived several years on three legs and while it is treatable, you can't cure it. Tripawds bear the brunt of chronic pain because they must alter their natural body mechanics to get around on three legs. It's similar to when a human walks with a limp; eventually the altered movement causes neck, shoulder, hip, and aches and pains. Likewise, if a dog's natural gait is altered over a lifetime, chronic pain intensifies. Conditions like osteoarthritis in Tripawds are a common result of chronic pain.

## What does chronic and acute pain look like?

It's not impossible to interpret our dog's pain language and body signals. Deciphering them is trial and error process, but if you suspect your dog might have pulled a muscle, needs better pain management after amputation surgery, or just seems off, consider these common signs of pain in pets. If any of them ring true for your Tripawd, it's time for a vet check-in.

Our friend Dr. Alex Avery of Our Pet's Health describes dog pain signals in more detail in this video.

❗ Video links from the <u>Tripawds Youtube Channel</u> available in premium ebook. Use Coupon Code BASIC10 for <u>$10 OFF the Tripawds Library</u>. See <u>https://tri.pet/teblib</u>

## Decreased activity

Does your dog seem "stubborn" on walks? We thought Jerry was being obstinate and just wanted to go home to eat dinner when he started turning around early while taking our after-work evening walks. The behavior came from out of left field, but we didn't see that he was telling us he hurt. Over the years, we've learned this happens a lot between pet parent and dog. What we *think* is laziness, old age, or stubbornness, is actually our dog telling us they hurt somewhere. If your dog suddenly refuses to go their normal distance of their usual walk, get them to the vet.

## Avoiding stairs

It's natural for new Tripawd dogs to be afraid of stairs right after surgery (especially open riser stairs). But if they once knew how to use stairs and then hesitate or stop altogether, something is wrong. Maybe they fell on the stairs when you weren't looking, maybe their hips or shoulders just hurt too much from the movement of using stairs. It's hard to say, but it's important to get your dog checked out by the vet.

## Reluctance to jump onto higher surfaces

First, you should know that rehabilitation therapists tell us that Tripawds shouldn't jump from high places to avoid putting stress on their joints. So please don't encourage your Tripawd to do that without training them to use pet stairs or furniture ramps. However, if you notice your pet hesitating to get onto furniture the way you taught them, or get into the car on their own, something is probably wrong.

## Slow to stand and sit

It's natural for pets to slow down somewhat as they age. But slowing down isn't always a sign of the aging process. Something is causing pain, whether it's existing chronic osteoarthritis or an acute new injury.

## Constantly licking the same body part

Obsessively grooming a specific body part is a sign that something's wrong. Gently palpate the area to look for wounds, burrs, thorns, or infection. Try to ice the area for a few minutes, a couple of times a day. If the behavior continues it's time for a vet visit.

## Weak appetite

For many dogs, this is one of the last ways of giving clues that they hurt. Some food-driven dogs will still eat, even when they are in excruciating pain. So you can't always use this as a pain signal. A weak appetite is just one piece of the puzzle of pain, but if you notice it in your dog, the first thing to do is to look in your pet's mouth. Do you notice signs of anything wrong, like a really foul smell, swollen gums, or bleeding? If nothing looks off, and feeding a yummy surprise treat doesn't help, call your vet.

"Pain is a very common cause of behavior changes in our dogs," explains Dr. Em, founder of The Vet Med Corner. She is a Canadian veterinarian looking to help spread research based information to all on YouTube and <u>on Facebook</u> too. "Most especially causing increases in anxiety, or jumpiness, or noise hypersensitivity."

In the following video, Dr. Em explains what subtle pain signals look like in dogs, and shares the differences between acute and chronic pain. She also discusses what to do if you suspect something is wrong but your dog isn't whining or crying. Watch as she answers these questions and more in this video all about dog pain.

**❗ All video links available in premium ebook. Use Coupon Code BASIC5 for <u>$5 OFF Premium E-book</u>. See <u>https://tri.pet/teb2</u>**

## What's the Best Way to Prevent Pain?

It's a great day when you get the "all clear!" by your vet after amputation sutures are removed. You might even be told that it's OK to resume all activity just like before, and maybe you'll give it a try that day. Who can blame you for wanting want to pick up where you left off? Returning to old routines is comforting. It helps us leave the mourning period of feeling sad that our dog lost a leg. Going to the dog park again, or just taking a long walk around the neighborhood feels like old times. And giving our dog a chance to do what they love again is one reason why we all opted for amputation surgery in the first place, right?

But before you grab the leash and head out the door, it's critical to know how to safely restart activity to protect your Tripawd from an injury. Unfortunately most veterinarians just don't have the time or knowledge to teach these things to us because they don't have a good idea of what your dog's activity was like at home before surgery. More importantly, unless the vet is a credentialed canine rehabilitation therapist, they usually have little to no training on safe movement and activity for three-legged dogs.

Sadly, many members turn to the Tripawds community for insight when their dog gets injured weeks or months after resuming activity. They often post in our <u>Hopping Around Discussion Forum</u>, to explain their dog's unusual behavior, like sitting down on walks. Or sometimes the dog can't walk at all.

## The Most Common Reasons for Pain and Injury After Amputation

If your dog was diagnosed with cancer and one morning they have difficulty getting around, it's easy to assume that maybe the disease has spread to other parts of the body. This is always a possibility, but usually the cause is something less sinister. In our experience, every situation is different, but more often tha not the typical cause of a three-legged dog's sudden mobility problem is over-activity. Usually, it's related to the duration and type of activities a dog is allowed to do after surgery, such as:

### Resuming old activity in exactly the same way

Usually by the time our veterinarian removes sutures and gives the OK to restart activity, our new Tripawd tends to look like they're able to keep doing what they did before surgery. And why shouldn't they? After all, the internet is filled with inspirational with videos and photos of amputee dogs running, chasing balls, and playing with other dogs! We are bombarded with messages of "Tripawds can do anything!" and it feels logical to assume our dog can too. But there's just one problem with that thinking. Those dogs we see on the internet are not *our* dog. They don't have our dog's unique physiology, age, body type, strength, etc. It's completely unfair to compare, and it leads to injuries.

We all want to get on with life and enjoy all the activities with our dog that we once did before. But most of us forget that our dog will do whatever it takes to keep up with everyone around them, even if it hurts them to try. So we let them resume their normal activity, and as a result, most new Tripawds experience muscle aches and soreness from getting too much of that activity, too soon after surgery.

This is the most common cause of preventable post-recovery pain new Tripawds experience, and it's not our fault. The majority of new Tripawd parents don't get specific veterinary guidance on how to safely restart activity for a new Tripawd. So if we've never gone thorough this experience before, and we've never had our dog evaluated by a canine rehabilitation therapist, how could we possibly know if our dog's usual activity is safe? How are we supposed to know what safe activity even looks like? Without professional guidance, most of us learn the hard way and our dog pays the price.

## Being a weekend warrior

Most dogs, Tripawds included, get minimal activity during the week while their people are at work. Between Monday and Friday, usually their only activity is a short evening walk or some yard play for a few minutes. But on weekends when it's time to go wild at the dog park, few limits are placed on the duration or intensity of the fun. Some Tripawds might play frisbee, chuck-it, or participate in high-impact sporting games like <u>AKC Fast CAT</u>. We won't deny that there's no greater joy than seeing your dog keep up with everyone else to do what they love, but the reality is that all of these scenarios are the perfect setup for an injury. It might take weeks or months to happen, but it's not at all uncommon for a new Tripawds member to report that after several months of everything being OK with their dog, an injury occurred and the dog needs a cruciate ligament repair or some other type of orthopedic surgery.

**! A Tripawd who participates in explosive, risky activities on the weekends without receiving ongoing, effective conditioning and strengthening exercises the rest of the week at great risk of a devastating (and expensive) injury.**

Although other situations can certainly provoke a remaining leg surgery, like being overweight, it's weekend warrior activities that most often put Tripawds out of commission.

## Being overweight

Did you know that every one pound of fat on a dog is the equivalent of five extra pounds of fat on a human? In other words, a dog who is only 5 pounds overweight is experiencing the same aches and pains as a person who is 25 pounds overweight. Only for the dogs, it's worse if they are missing a leg. Nobody ever expects their dog to lose a leg. Those overweight dogs who do lose a leg while carrying extra weight will have more challenges to regain mobility after amputation surgery. Once they do recover, that extra weight puts an extra burden on their body that is already compensating for the missing leg.

**! All Tripawds who carry extra weight are at risk of painful and expensive <u>remaining leg surgeries</u>.**

The good news is that we are the ones who control what our dogs eat. Their weight is in our hands, and there are plenty of things we can do to help dogs lose weight safely. The Diet and Nutrition Chapter in our book explains more.

There is nothing more upsetting than to see your dog survive recovery and feel better, only to get hurt and unable to do what they love. It makes you question the very reason why you decided to amputate in the first place. That's exactly what happened to us as we learned the hard way with Jerry and Wyatt. And we see this happen to most new Tripawds parents too. This struggle is real, and the lack of specific veterinary guidance most of us receive on discharge day is a serious problem. Even the most dog-savvy pet parent has difficulty judging what is safe and appropriate activity for a Tripawd dog. We live with a never-ending guessing game that sometimes ends with muscle strains, joint stress, and chronic mobility problems that are expensive to treat and lower quality of life.

Deciding on the right type and length of activity for your Tripawd is a tightrope act. You'll constantly learn from your mistakes, but you can minimize them by taking advantage of the <u>Tripawds Rehab Reimbursement Program</u>. A rehabilitation therapist is the best veterinary professional to guide you in this journey. Take your Tripawd to see one, and the Tripawds Foundation can pay up to $200 for that first consultation. There is no better way to learn what safe exercise looks like, and how to keep your Tripawd injury free.

## Work with Your Veterinarian to Identify Your Dog's Pain

If your Tripawd is showing pain signals, the best thing you can do to help your vet decide on next steps is to take out your smart phone and start taking video of their movements. Record your dog walking from a front, rear, and sideways view. Catch them on camera when they get up from the floor. Bookmark the clips so they're handy during your appointment. Next, fill out the following pain-scoring chart.

### Pinpoint Pain with a Pain Scoring Chart

Pain scoring charts help us rate pain in a visual way, so that we can have a better conversation with our veterinary team. Many exist in the veterinary and human medical world, and the BEAP

Pain Signal Charts are one of our favorites for pet parents to use. BEAP charts use basic cues in eight areas to help us determine if our pet is experiencing discomfort, and the level of pain being experienced by our pet. "BEAP" is an acronym for the eight areas that include:

**B**   Breathing: is it normal? Fast? Too slow?

**E**   Eyes: are they bright and alert, or dull and worried?

**A**   Ambulation: is any lameness present on walks?

**A**   Activity: do you see playful behavior, or reluctance to engage?

**A**   Appetite: are they frisky or finicky about their usual food?

**A**   Attitude: can you see happy or anxious behavior?

**P**   Posture: does your dog sit up tall, or scrunched and hunched?

**P**   Palpation: what happens when you run your hands gently along their body?

Remember, you know your pet the best. You can see the subtle changes and behaviors on a daily basis. As you watch, keep in mind two important things:

1.   **Pain is dynamic.** Symptoms can fluctuate from day to day, even hour to hour. It can also depend on what kind of activity your Tripawd was doing just prior to the painful event.

2.   **Pain can mimic many other diseases.** Don't automatically assume your pet is in pain just because your pet experiences some of these symptoms. It's important to note the symptoms and discuss with your vet.

## Pinpointing pain in a clinical setting

In a perfect world, our veterinarian would come to our house to watch our dog's behavior and observe for signs of pain.

Unfortunately most of us aren't lucky enough to have a vet who makes house calls. The moment we step into an exam room, our dog's personality can drastically change. With so many smells, activity, and unfriendly memories flooding their brain, most dogs do not get comfortable enough in a veterinary clinic to reveal how they are really feeling. Pinpointing the source of pain in an exam room is tough for even the best vets.

► Your videos, BEAP charts, thorough notes, and total honesty about your dog's activity level at home are important tools during the exam that can help your Tripawd feel better faster. Give your veterinary team a complete picture of what's happening at home so they can diagnose sooner.

At the exam, your vet will spend time palpating your dog's suspected painful areas, and possibly recommend diagnostic tests based on the symptoms they are seeing. But sometimes, an on-the-spot diagnosis just isn't possible. It's uncommon to leave with a "wait and see" plan by your vet. They'll prescribe pain medication, and strict orders for your dog to take it easy for a couple of weeks. Quite often that's enough to resolve the problem. However, if your vet gives you the wait-and-see recommendation, don't leave the clinic without a Plan B.

Questions you'll want to have ready before you even get to the clinic include:

► Is there anything else we can do today to find out what's going on?
► How long should we give the symptoms to go away?
► What can I do to help with the pain while we wait? Is icing appropriate? How long and how often?
► What kind of activity should my dog avoid while we wait? How far can they go for a walk? Can they play with other dogs?
► If my dog doesn't get better, what are the next steps to consider?
► Should I just see a specialist now? Why or why not? If yes, can you recommend one?

While you wait patiently and follow the treatment plan, it could help to have your dog evaluated by a canine rehabilitation therapist. These experts are pros and pinpointing pain and can often do it much sooner than general practice veterinarians.

Consider booking an appointment with a therapist. Be sure to describe the urgency of your dog's mobility situation so you can hopefully get them in sooner.

## Advocate for your dog: seek a second opinion if necessary.

Most of us have "white coat syndrome" in a medical setting, deferring everything to the veterinary team without question. But when it comes to treating pain, being a firm but polite advocate for our Tripawd is critical. A three-legged dog is more likely to end up at the vet clinic for pain than other dogs, so it's in their best interest for us to learn how to be better advocates as early as possible in the journey. Oftentimes we will spend a lot of money on pain relief and diagnostics before we get frustrated enough to seek help elsewhere. Don't let this happen to you!

Be patient and follow through with your vet's first treatment plan. If your dog doesn't improve within that time frame, and the next treatment plan is not helping either, get a second opinion from another vet. A great vet will connect you with a colleague at another practice on request. Or they may also refer out to a specialist who can hopefully pinpoint the problem, whether it's an orthopedic or neurologist practitioner. If you have access to a board-certified veterinary surgeon and/or sports medicine and rehabilitation practitioner (ACVS, ACVSMR), that's even better!

A second opinion from another vet might seem like an extra expense that you can't afford. But in the long run that second opinion will save you money. Your dog will be also spared from the undue pain and stress of an untreated injury and your finances will be saved from the cost of tests and medications that aren't leading to a diagnosis.

## How to Manage Pain and Injuries

Many of us are reluctant to give our dog more pain medication. We fear that our dog will live in a dopey haze with low quality of life, and worry that our dogs can get "hooked" on narcotics. The reality is that while pain medications can sedate a dog, just like they do with people, dogs don't wrestle with addiction issues the way humans do. Just like with their diet, we control how much medication they get, and we can help them gently ease off medication when it's time. But meanwhile, when any animal is physically hurting, prescription pain control is the fastest way to temporarily resolve it until the root cause can be identified and treated so pain does not return. And while medication usually isn't the only modality that is needed, it's the most important one.

Just as all dogs are different, every veterinarian approaches pain management a little differently, based on their successes with other dogs in similar situations. The best vets follow current guidelines for standards of practice:

▶ American Animal Hospital Association (AAHA) Pain Management Guidelines
▶ World Small Animal Veterinary Association (WSAVA) Global Pain Council Guidelines.

How do you know if your vet follows them? Just ask. But be sure to inquire with the appreciation and respect that highly trained veterinarians deserve.

## Commonly Used Pain Medications for Acute and Chronic Pain

Resolving your Tripawd's pain depends on your dog's physiology, a little trial-and-error of medications, and hands-on rehabilitation therapy treatments like massage, acupuncture, cold laser therapy, and others.

Medications that work for post-surgery acute pain might not work for chronic pain, and vice versa. Your vet will prescribe pain medications such as Meloxicam, Gabapentin, Amantadine, Methocarbamol, or others. A combination of different types can attack it from different pain pathways, helping to resolve it sooner.

The most common "gold standard" pain medications recommended by AAHA and WSAVA for acute and chronic pain in dogs include:

## Non-Steroidal Anti-Inflammatories (NSAIDs)

Pain is a major cause of inflammation in muscles and tissues in the body. The inflammation causes swelling, hot-to-the-touch areas, and makes life miserable. Vets prescribe Carprophen, Meloxicam, and Previcox to bring acute, sudden inflammatory pain under control. When taken on a long-term basis, NSAIDs can safely manage long-term inflammation caused by conditions like osteoarthritis. Another benefit illustrated by a few veterinary studies is that NSAIDs may slow the growth of cancer cells and prevent tumors from growing – something especially helpful for dogs fighting cancer!

NSAIDs (like all medications) have some risk of side-effects. A small number of dogs may experience gastrointestinal upset, kidney, or liver function disruption (usually it's when a dog has other commodities (illnesses) affecting those organs). Despite the risk, many studies looking at the safety profile of NSAIDs show that they are still one of the safest and most effective medications to treat inflammation in dogs.

Your veterinarian will try to prevent any side-effects by ordering a complete blood chemistry (CBC) panel. This test ensures all organs are healthy and functioning. If side effects do happen, it's usually in the first two to four weeks of use.

Watch for signs like:
► Decrease or increase in appetite
► Vomiting
► Change in bowel movements (such as diarrhea, or black, tarry, or bloody stools)
► Change in behavior (such as decreased or increased activity level, incoordination, seizure or aggression)
► Yellowing of gums, skin, or whites of the eyes (jaundice)
► Change in drinking habits (frequency, amount consumed)
► Change in urination habits (frequency, color, or smell)
► Change in skin (redness, scabs, or scratching)

## What if Your Dog Can't Tolerate NSAIDs?

An osteoarthritis pain relief medication known as Galliprant is a good alternative for dogs who can't tolerate NSAIDs. It's a type of anti-inflammatory that doesn't come with the same side effect risks as typical NSAID medications. According to its manufacturer, Galliprant treats chronic pain related to osteoarthritis.

## Does Long-Term Use of NSAIDs Cause Side-Effects in Dogs?

According to veterinarians, there is no evidence showing that long-term use of NSAIDs puts a dog at risk of side-effects. "We want to use the safest medications that we can," says veterinary pain management expert Dr. Tamara Grubb. "And that's why for some of the medications, like the anti-inflammatory drugs, we as a veterinarian might ask you to come back in more often for blood work than you used to. To come in just so we can be sure that the drug is still safe for your pet and that it's still working."

### Adjunctive Pain Medications

Certain drugs used in human and veterinary medicine are known as "adjunctive" pain medications. This class of drugs includes Gabapentin, Amantadine, and Methocarbamol, three commonly prescribed to new Tripawds for acute and chronic pain. They are not as powerful or fast acting as NSAIDs, but they attack the pain differently and complement how the NSAIDs work in the body. They are also well-studied and proven to be safe for humans, but have few scientific studies behind them for veterinary use. However, the anecdotal evidence on their effectiveness for treating pain is strong enough to convince most veterinarians to prescribe them "off-label" for effective relief, at least until the research proves otherwise.

### Gabapentin

Also known by its brand name, Neurontin, Gabapentin is an anti-seizure drug that vets use in people and animals before and after amputation surgery. It can keep the body's nerves from "winding up" in reaction to surgery pain. By preventing wind-up pain, Gabapentin helps humans and animals experience less pain after surgery. This medication can successfully treat neuropathic pain (the burning and tingling sensations that come from damaged nerves), and in many human studies has been shown to help minimize post-amputation phantom limb pain, manage osteoarthritis pain, and reduce nerve pain caused by an acute injury.

This medication is safe and gentle on the liver, but may not be suitable for all animals with elevated kidney levels. Vets can prescribe it in a wide range of dosages to suit an animal's size and pain control needs. Many start with a small dose after surgery, and bump it up from there if it seems like a new Tripawd's pain is not being controlled. More often than not, the dosage needs adjusting to the individual patient's needs. Pain experts like Dr. Mike Petty DVM tell us that Gabapentin is as effective when prescribed on an "as-needed" basis, but when given over time, can be more effective to help your dog's body cope with chronic pain.

Like any medication, Gabapentin can have side effects, which are generally not serious and not enough to discontinue use before the pain is resolved. Possible side effects of Gabapentin in dogs may include:
- Sedation, Sleepiness, or Lethargy
- Occasional Vomiting
- Lack of coordination

**How to Make Gabapentin Work for Your Dog:**
- First, tell your vet about all medications, supplements, and cannabis (CBD) products your pet is taking before you give the first dose. Some medications, like antacids, can decrease the effectiveness of Gabapentin. This medication can lower blood pressure, and since cannabis can do the same, it's important to let your vet know if your dog is getting it.
- Gabapentin can cause sedation. Ask your vet to prescribe a low starting dose. Start with a smaller dosage in the morning and higher one at night. This will help your dog acclimate to the sedative effects, which will decrease over time.
- Dosages often need to be fine-tuned if a dog is too sedated, or it appears the pain isn't under control. Ask your vet to prescribe Gabapentin in 100 mg capsules, so that you and your vet can easily fine-tune the dosage if necessary. Smaller dosages also help to minimize sedation effects by slowly building up the dose while your dog's body gets used to the sedation.
- Giving Gabapentin with food is helpful for dogs with sensitive stomachs. Pets with liver disease and some with elevated kidney levels may be able to use it too, but with close monitoring.

▶ DO NOT suddenly stop giving Gabapentin, especially if your dog has taken it for more than a few weeks. Eliminating it without a slow withdrawal can cause severe "wind-up pain" that's hard to bring down under control. This medication should be gradually withdrawn by decreasing the dosage and frequency over a week or two. Ask your vet for guidance.

▶ **WARNING! Double-check you are using the veterinary version of Gabapentin.** The human version of Gabapentin in liquid form contains Xylitol, which is toxic to pets. If you get your pet's prescriptions from a human pharmacy. Never get the human version of Gabapentin. Xylitol is found in the liquid form only.

❗ Gabapentin is also known by many brand names around the world including: Adekin, Amanta, Amantagamma, Amantan, Amantrel, Amixx, Antadine, Antiflu-DES, Atarin, Atenegine, Cerebramed, Endantadine, Infectoflu, Influ-A, Lysovir, Mantadine, Mantadix, Mantidan, Padiken, Symadine,Viroifral and Virucid.

## Pregabalin

Similar to Gabapentin, this anti-epileptic medication also known as Lyrica in human medicine, is now being prescribed by some veterinarians as a better source of nerve pain relief than Gabapentin. It acts on pain receptors exactly the same way, and has the same sedative side effect, but is more potent and more predictable with its response. And unlike Gabapentin, it doesn't require as high of a dosage to see clinical effects. According to one Pregabalin study, it has the potential to provide better pain relief in fewer doses.

So if Gabapentin is not working for your Tripawd, Pregabalin is worth discussing with your veterinarian. Your pet can start taking it right away, because it doesn't require a "washout" period to switch from one to the other.

However, you may receive some pushback if you ask for it. The reason is that Pregabalin is more costly than Gabapentin. It also classified as a controlled substance, so some veterinarians may not be enthusiastic about prescribing it.

This is where advocating for your dog is more important than ever to give the pain relief they deserve. Good resources you may want to discuss include:

▸ Pregabalin for the treatment of syringomyelia-associated neuropathic pain in dogs: A randomised, placebo-controlled, double-masked clinical trial
▸ Effects of Pregabalin on Dogs, Clinician's Brief

## Amantadine

Many veterinarians will add Amantadine into the mix when a Gabapentin and NSAID combination doesn't control pain. This drug is used for Parkinson's disease in humans, while showing good evidence that it can reduce pain by changing the brain's response to it. Tripawds member and volunteer veterinarian in our discussion forums, Dr. Pam Wilztius says that "Amantadine helps prevent what is called pain 'wind up.' Once the pain receptors are annoyed it takes more pain meds to calm them down. This drug blocks that response and can be used for 1-2 weeks post op. Lots of dogs with chronic arthritis also take this drug for flare-ups when the Rimadyl or other NSAIDs they are taking stop working."

According to VeterinaryPartner.com, when Amantadine is used alone it is not an effective analgesic, nor as fast-acting. But when combined with other pain relievers, and ideally when given twice daily, it can help ease pain, decrease stress and lower anxiety, the two most common behaviors that Tripawds in pain experience.

Amantadine has a good safety profile and minimal chance of side effects. Some effects seen can include diarrhea, flatulence, and agitation. In humans, it reportedly has caused hallucinations, dizziness, and other forms of mental health disruption. This has not been documented in dogs.

## Ketamine

In some cases of chronic, long-term pain caused by osteoarthritis, your vet might want to start your dog on low dose injections of a surgical anesthesia drug called Ketamine. For decades this low-cost anesthetic drug has been used in human and veterinary medicine surgeries. Today's experts are learning that regular, low dose Ketamine injections can help dogs with osteoarthritis too.

It does this by stimulating neuroplasticity, which is the process of re-training the brain to adapt to changing needs in the body.

"Ketamine is such a powerful component of pain relief when added to other analgesics that consensus statements for its use in humans with both acute and chronic pain have been developed," says <u>Dr. Tamara Grubb</u>. When given in low dose treatments, ketamine not only relieves pain but simultaneously changes the brain's response to pain. The result creates a new "map" that teaches the brain how to perceive pain. An added benefit is that it can help chronically painful dogs sleep better, without the side effects of opioids.

Despite the powerful effect Ketamine offers, in low doses it's extremely safe. <u>Ketamine works in dogs</u> just minutes after the first injection. Dogs can receive in the clinic, or for dogs who don't do well in that setting, can receive via a small wearable device that releases small amounts over a day or two. It is metabolized by the liver and excreted by kidneys, and has very low risk of side effects. However dogs with any form of heart, kidney, or liver disease, hypertension, seizures, or larynx disorders should not take it.

## Methocarbamol

Technically, Methocarbamol (also known as Robaxin in both human and veterinary medicine) is not a pain reliever but a <u>skeletal muscle relaxant</u>. When used in conjunction with the above pain relievers, it can provide faster pain relief for severe pain from injuries or inflammation of the muscles, ligaments, tendons, and muscle spasms before or after surgery

"Researchers believe that methocarbamol is able to dampen or decrease the abnormal signals, which helps relieve the muscle tremors or spasms," writes Dr. Julie Buzby, DVM. In her article <u>"Methocarbamol for Dogs (Robaxin): What it is and How it's Used,</u>" she says "Yet the methocarbamol doesn't affect the ability of the neurons to send the signals necessary for normal muscle tone and muscle contraction. This means that therapeutic doses can often relieve spasms without significantly affecting a dog's ability to walk."

Like many medications, methocarbamol can have sedative effects in some dogs, and possibly some drooling or nausea. In some it can cause occasional increases in cardiac rate, and decreases in blood pressure, which doesn't make it a great choice for dogs with heart conditions or those taking a cannabis product (which can also lower blood pressure). Experts say that slow decreases from Methocarbamol are kinder on the body than sudden withdrawal.

## Tramadol: Just Say No.

For decades, veterinarians believed that Tramadol could help dogs cope with amputation pain. But this landmark 2018 Tramadol study changed everything. It found that Tramadol is not as effective in controlling major acute pain, and today's vets who practice modern pain management no longer turn to it.

▶ Veterinary pain management expert Dr. Robin Downing, DVM, DAIPM, DACVSMR, CVPP, CCRP explains on Tripawd Talk Radio episode #96.

In our Tripawds News article, The Best Dog and Cat Amputation Pain Medications, board-certified veterinary surgeon Dr. Stephen Jones, MVB, MS, DACVS-SA, DECVS (Diplomate, American College of Veterinary Surgery – Small Animal and Diplomate of the European College of Veterinary Surgery), agrees. "Gone are the days where we just give dogs and NSAID and Tramadol and send them home," he shared. "To that end, it bears mentioning that we no longer believe that Tramadol provides any significant pain control in pets. A nice study came out of the University of Georgia a few years ago (Budsburg et al.) that showed Tramadol does not provide any major benefit as part of a pain control protocol in dogs."

Despite the significant evidence that Tramadol does not work for amputation surgery pain, too many Tripawds are still coming home with this unhelpful medication. If your vet prescribes it to your dog for amputation pain, please advocate for a stronger medication (like the ones mentioned here, such as Gabapentin and NSAID medication. Your dog's comfort is in your hands. The best recoveries start with the best pain relief.

## Tapentadol (Possibly an option, but hard to find)

This opioid is a newer, more effective version of Tramadol that complements the effects of NSAIDs and Gabapentin. A 2021 Tramadol versus Tapentadol analysis of existing research concluded that "Tapentadol might have a superior analgesic profile in animals, but the effectiveness of this opioid needs to be further clarified before recommending its use for managing acute and chronic pain in dogs and cats."

Unfortunately, as of this writing Tapentadol is just starting to get studied in veterinary medicine, and many vets aren't using it yet. However, if other pain relief doesn't help, it's worth mentioning to your vet as an alternative to Tramadol.

## Acetaminophen with Codeine

**This has taken the place of Fentanyl, as a result of the opiod crisis.** Some veterinarians will prescribe this combo for dogs who cannot tolerate NSAIDs, or as part of a post-amputation pain management therapy. Many studies like this 2020 study (albeit with a very small sample size) show this is not always an effective choice as the sole method of pain control.

### Other Ways to Manage Chronic Pain

Whether you have a front leg amputee or rear leg amputee, the long-term physiological effects of amputation are predictable. No Tripawd is immune to problems caused by an altered gait. Even if your dog is extremely fit, it's likely they will still experience chronic pain at some point in their life. When that happens, one or more types of chronic pain relief medications may be prescribed, such as:

## Librela (Anti-NGF Monoclonal Antibody Therapy) for Osteoarthritis

This is an "anti-nerve growth factor (NGF) monoclonal antibody treatment" for osteoarthritis pain in dogs. It works by using a dog's naturally occurring antibodies to reduce inflammation and pain. The therapy has been used in human medicine since about 2020, and was approved for use in American veterinary medicine in May 2023 (but has been used in Europe a few years longer).

Librela is a monthly injection medication given at the vet clinic. It's not meant as a substitute for an NSAID like Meloxicam, but to complement it. And it doesn't cure osteoarthritis, so you'll need to continue providing excellent joint support to your dog.

Anti-NGF monoclonal antibody therapy is just beginning to be understood and practiced in human and veterinary medicine. How it works is not entirely understood, so be aware that like any new therapy, certain side effects of Librela may be seen in a small number of dogs taking it.

A growing number of veterinarians are suggesting to use Librela as a last resort. "According to Indiana veterinarian Daniel Beatty, DVM, CAC, CVA, CERP, "Librela was not designed for use in dogs with spinal arthritis or other painful neurologic conditions. Use with caution in any dog with neurologic symptoms such as weakness, incoordination, ataxia, or proprioception deficits."

## Adequan Canine

The Adequan Canine medication has been around for almost 10 years. It's not a supplement, it's a drug that must be prescribed by your vet. As of today it's the only FDA-approved cartilage-protecting treatment that helps dogs get better by treating the disease, not just symptoms. Adequan has the scientific research behind it to prove it restores joint lubrication, relieves inflammation, and renews the building blocks of healthy cartilage.

The most effective way to benefit from Adequan Canine is to prescribe it early, before cartilage wears away completely. But even if it's not, Adequan may help reduce an arthritic dog's pain, and enable them to enjoy increased activity. This medication is first given as a "loading dose" injection, twice a week for up to four weeks (maximum of 8 injections). After that, it can be given at a "maintenance" dose of weekly, bi-weekly, or monthly, depending on the dog.

## Stem Cell Therapy and Platelet Rich Plasma (Regenerative Medicine)

This pain management option is not a medication like those above, but rather a long-term therapy. The most simplified way to describe how Regenerative Medicine works, is that it's the process of extracting specific cells from a patient's blood. The cells get processed in a certain way, then re-injected back into the patient. The goal is to produce naturally-occurring substances in the body to help promote healing and reduce inflammation. Evidence of its efficacy has been building for at least two decades, with the strongest evidence showing that it can give pain relief for some dogs with osteoarthritis. When used alongside other therapies, regenerative medicine can be a good way to reduce chronic pain in certain dogs.

@tripawds

The problem with regenerative medicine is that results can vary widely among dogs. And unfortunately, it's not an inexpensive treatment; costs can reach well over $2,000 for the initial course. Lacking hard <u>regenerative medicine evidence</u> showing that it definitely works (or doesn't), many veterinarians are reluctant to recommend it as a first-line, long-term pain relief choice.

## What About Natural Remedies for Pain Management?

Veterinary pain management has come a long way since our Jerry lost his leg in 2006. Today's animals can feel pain relief faster and more effectively than ever before, because we have more treatment choices than ever. But unfortunately, many "natural" pain remedies, including homeopathy or "CBD" cannabis products, should <u>never</u> be a first line treatment after a major surgery like amputation, or when your dog has a joint or muscle injury. Here's why:

## Homeopathy

In the early days of the Tripawds community, we tried to be open-minded about this therapy, and included a few articles about <u>homeopathic remedies in the Tripawds Nutrition blog</u>. But since then we have changed our position to align with evidence-based veterinary experts who agree, homeopathy is not effective for treating pain. Nearly all human medical associations and most major veterinary associations around the world agree, including the Australian Veterinary Association, British Veterinary Association, and the Royal College of Veterinary Surgeons. They all acknowledge that this 18th-century therapy is ineffective and has no place in medicine. The American Veterinary Medical Association continues <u>the homeopathy debate</u>.

Despite the lack of evidence for it, homeopathy continues to be practiced by many integrative veterinarians striving to use more "natural" ways to help their animal clients with pain and other health issues.

Homeopathy is based upon the theory of the "law of similars," which says that a substance capable of causing particular symptoms in a healthy individual will cure similar symptoms in a person with disease. The "medication" is a diluted form of that substance, given to the patient whose body will theoretically react and fight the disease or condition "naturally."

Unfortunately over 200 years after it was popularized in 18th century medicine, homeopathic practitioners have never been able to concretely prove that this therapy actually works. Nor have they ever been able to prove that it's any different than giving a patient a placebo. As a consequence, most major veterinary and human medical associations have statements opposed to treating animals or humans with homeopathy.

## Cannabis (CBD)

If you've ever reached for a CBD pet product, you are buying something made with the cannabis plant. Sure, everyone calls it "CBD" but let's give this plant the respect it deserves. CBD is just one of nearly 200 molecules in leaves of hemp and marijuana cannabis plants that can help with problems ranging from epilepsy to pain. So let's start by using this plant's proper name – cannabis.

We could write entire chapter about cannabis. For the purposes of this book, we are going to summarize what we feel are the most important things you need to know about cannabis veterinary medicine.

As you can see in our Cannabis Corner articles in Tripawds News, we are very much in favor of science-based approaches to using cannabis medicine for pets and people. Ever year, more legitimate studies are showing that cannabis can be safely used to treat conditions like pain in dogs. But cannabis is not always as successful or safe as marketing messages want us to believe.

## Cannabis is **not** a first line pain relief treatment.

Nobody wants to see their dog in pain or pump them full of chemicals. But if you suspect your dog is in pain, **never** reach for cannabis before a prescription pain medication. The main reason is that unlike 99% of cannabis products being sold, prescription drugs are tested for safety, effectiveness, and predictability. Treat your dog's pain quickly, then explore cannabis once it's under control. Or, if your dog is still hurting and vet team has tried everything – and you are working with a veterinary cannabis expert knowledgeable about cannabis medicine – then of course it makes sense to incorporate cannabis to try to help your dog feel better.

We understand that using natural therapies can be more appealing than pharmaceuticals. But please don't worry about your dog getting hooked on pain pills, or having withdrawals. Neither has been proven to happen in dogs. Yes, there are ways to treat pain with cannabis as effectively and reliably as most prescription pain medications, but it takes a lot of trial-and-error with an expert practitioner. Get the pain under control, then give it ia try if you want to do it.

**❗ Please never use any cannabis product instead of a prescription pain medication, or add it to your dog's veterinary medications without letting your vet team know. Keep reading to find out why this is so important.**

## Most CBD pet products are garbage.

Cannabis medicine is generally safe for most pets and people. The problem is that government regulation overseeing cannabis products contain is weak. In the US, there is no single agency that can guarantee these products contain what they say is on their label. The Food and Drug Administration oversees cannabis product regulations. And every year, the FDA announces more studies proving that poorly made cannabis products flooding the marketplace. Many cannabis products contain contaminants, like heavy metals. Others don't even have the amounts of cannabis molecules like CBD that they claim to have!

In this article, How to Avoid Toxic CBD Pet Products, we share some important tips on selecting quality cannabis products for pets.

**❗ When used with expert help, a good cannabis product can help bring the body into balance.**

## Many cannabis products contain toxins.

Did you know that cannabis plants are used to clean up contaminated soil? That's because this plant is good at "bio-accumulation." It does a great job absorbing all of the elements in soils where it is grown. This means that if a cannabis plant grows in toxic soils, it will absorb those toxins. If a grower sprays pesticides, the plant will absorb that too. And ultimately, it will pass all of the toxins into whatever product the plant evolves into. Ingesting those toxins is defeating the purpose of healing, especially for cancer patients.

**How to Spot Toxins in Cannabis Products**

As consumers who only want to help our pets feel better, we are doing right by our dog if we know exactly what is inside a product. The best way to do this is by obtaining a Certificate of Analysis (COA) from whatever company you are looking into.

▶ Every reputable cannabis product maker will have a COA for each product they sell, even treats.

▶ The COA should be no more than 1 year old, and ideally no more than 6 months old.

▶ A quality COA will show which cannabis molecules are in the product, and how much of each the product contains. It will also show the product has been tested for heavy metals, fungus, and pesticides.

Unfortunately, only a small number of cannabis manufacturers go to the trouble and expense of bi-annually testing their products. They're out there, but you have to search for them. If you are interested in a cannabis product and you aren't seeing a link to a current COA, ask the company for it. And if they won't provide one to you, shop elsewhere.

**!** If your selected cannabis manufacturer does not provide a COA for their product, find another brand or seek a professional opinion. Do not ask for recommendations on social media.

## Cannabis can negatively impact some canine health conditions.

Dogs with medical conditions like heart disease, or those taking medications like Gabapentin or Amantadine, can experience extreme sedation or low blood pressure, even with products that do not contain the THC molecule that causes the "high" marijuana is known for. Young dogs who haven't stopped growing can also be impacted, because their endocannabinoid system is not fully developed. Known as the "ECS," it keeps our nervous and immune systems in balance. Cannabis works directly on the ECS, and without a fully-grown system, the exchange may prevent healthy development. Want to learn more? This article explains <u>how cannabis works</u> in the body.

Many veterinarians are selling cannabis products in their lobby. The manufacturer <u>ElleVet</u> is one of the most popular choices veterinarians are making, and thankfully they produce one of the most reputable cannabis therapy lines. However, be aware that just because the bottle dosage works well for one dog of exactly the same weight as yours, it probably won't work the same way in your dog. This is because cannabis impacts a body differently based on the needs of a patient's health circumstances and their ECS.

We will repeat: it is critical to work with a veterinarian who understands cannabis medicine. Not only will you help your pet feel better sooner, but you won't be wasting money on ineffective products.

Dr. Gary Richter provides a clear overview of cannabis use for pets in this video.

❗ All video links available in premium ebook. Use Coupon Code BASIC5 for <u>$5 OFF Premium E-book</u>. See <u>https://tri.pet/teb2</u>

## Work with an Expert to Pick Cannabis Products

Finding the right cannabis product and dosage to make your Tripawd feel better takes time and expertise. Once you choose a veterinary cannabis expert, they will run a full CBC blood panel to confirm how your dog's body is functioning. Then they will recommend a proper cannabis product with what they believe is a good combination of molecules to treat your dog's pain. It may take weeks of trial and error to achieve the goal. But with patience, the goal can be achieved. We see it all the time for conditions ranging from skin allergies to seizure disorders to severe chronic pain.

Natural cannabis products are not one-size-fits-all. Just as your dog is unique, so is their physiology. Cannabis therapy can work across different mammalian species, but how it works is different for every body. That is why we cannot say it enough: please do not replace your veterinarian's prescribed drugs with any cannabis pet products that you purchase – or especially a product that a friend swears works great on their dog. At best you may be depriving your pet of fast, effective, and safe pain relief treatments proven to be safe and more helpful. And at worst, you could cause more problems like low blood pressure, or give your dog a toxic soup of heavy metals.

Every year scientists are learning new ways to use it more effectively to treat pain and other ailments. But until you know exactly what kind of product you are getting, and working alongside a veterinarian who can help you make the most of that product,

## Find a Veterinary Cannabis Expert

Veterinary Cannabis Society Directory of Practitioners

Veterinary Cannabis Education and Referral Services

CHAPTER 5
# The Benefits of Canine Rehab Therapy

After surgery, we are all eager to let our new Tripawd get back to the business of being a dog. Most of us assume our dog will strengthen in time, build up the ability to go on long walks again, and "self-regulate" by letting us know when they want to take a break. But the truth is, our dogs cannot do any of this without our help. Sure, they will try to do what they did before. And they might even succeed for a while. But the reality is that too many new Tripawds do too much too soon, and eventually get injured because their human doesn't know how to build up to safe activity, or what to look for when they've had too much of a good thing. We see it over and over again, and it's one reason why you will always hear us talking about why a Tripawd needs rehabilitation therapy.

When Tripawds founder Jerry had his leg removed in 2006, the canine rehabilitation field hardly existed. It wasn't until he got injured that his oncologist suggested we take him to rehab therapy. We were shocked to learn that just like in human medicine, dogs can also benefit from guided, safe exercises to help them resume activity and stay injury free. And over the years we have learned that dogs who get at least a few weeks of rehabilitation therapy after surgery will do better than those who do not.

Dogs who get evaluated by an expert always do better because in the process of receiving rehab. And, their human can learn things like:
► Where the dog is weak, or strong
► How to address pain issues resulting from becoming a Tripawd
► The best exercises and stretching to help their dog prepare for a new life on three legs
► What safe activity looks like for their dog, and how to resume it
► How to watch for pain signals after activity
► And what do do if pain is suspected

We believe so strongly in the benefits of rehab therapy, that the Tripawds Rehab Grant program can pay for your first consultation with a certified practitioner.

❗ See what Tripawds Parents Have to Say About Rehab Therapy in testimonials from Tripawds Rehab Grant recipients. **See: https://tripawds.org/tag/rehab**

Without expert rehab therapy guidance, a Tripawd parent is completely unaware of the harmful effects of certain activities they allow their three-legged dogs to do. Even if their dog is getting around fine today, the pet parent doesn't realize why or how their dog is at risk of a future injury. When it happens, life comes to a standstill and the emotional turmoil from living through that amputation decision comes back.

But it's not just Tripawds who benefit from rehab therapy. Dr. Jessica Waldman of California Animal Rehabilitation Center in Los Angeles says if she could she all of her rehab patients when they are young, healthy puppies, she would warn their humans about the dangers of certain activities. For instance, allowing a dog to jump in and out of vehicles, or fly down steps, or participate in explosive activity without warming up and cooling down are all activities that put a dog at risk of injuries like a cranial cruciate ligament tear. Waldman says she would tell pet parents to train their dog to use a step or ramp when getting onto furniture or in and out of cars. And when it comes to Tripawds, she says she would remind all pet parents that their three-legged dog should never walk longer than 20 minutes at a time without a break.

If we don't think about canine rehabilitation and injury prevention until *after* our dog has experienced a major trauma like amputation, retraining behavior is tough for the parent and the pet. It's a frustrating experience added to a distressing time in our lives when going through amputation surgery recovery. Unfortunately the majority of pet parents don't know this information. Even when an injury happens to a four or three-legged dog, a discussion about the benefits of canine rehabilitation is often left out of the conversations between veterinarian and pet parent.

In some cases this might be because a dog isn't projected to live longer than the cancer prognosis. But this is totally unfair to the dog because cancer rarely behaves exactly as it's "supposed" to. Many dogs with cancer will outlive their prognosis. Our Jerry lived a happy life on three legs for two years when doctors gave him a prognosis of only six to eight months!

As Trouble's mom once told us, no dog has an expiration date stamped on their butt! Whether a dog is fighting cancer or lost a leg for other reasons, rehabilitation therapy should be a mandatory part of learning how to navigate the world on three legs, together. Not only will you have a good time together doing it, but your three-legged hero will achieve optimal health and strength for a lifetime.

## What Rehab Therapy Can Do for Your Tripawd

Rehab therapy (also known as "physio") is a critical part of caring for a Tripawd. More veterinary schools are including a small amount of rehab therapy education in their curriculum, but most practicing vets at this time still don't have training in canine rehabilitation therapy or have a good understanding of its benefits. But as you can see in the Tripawds Foundation News Blog, the benefits of rehabilitation therapy for amputee dogs is very clear.

We see the benefits more than the average general practice veterinarian does, simply because more three-legged animals walk through our virtual doors than a typical veterinary practice. This is a huge reason why the Tripawds Foundation will pay for any Tripawd's first rehabilitation therapy evaluation.

That first visit is so educational for us! We can learn where our dog is strong or weak, and how to watch for potential problems. A rehab therapist can inform us about injury prevention and then show how to lead strengthening and endurance-building activities at home on our own. The best part is, we all have fun doing it!

! At the heart and soul of the Tripawds Foundation is our mission to help our three-legged heroes live fit, healthy lives. Rehab therapy is the best way to start. So please, apply for the Maggie Moo Fund for Tripawd Rehab and see how much happier your hero is because you took this important step!

Rehab therapy isn't just helpful for older Tripawds or those with cancer. It's for all three-legged dogs because without that spare leg, a dog loses the ability to tolerate a normal level of activity as a four-legged dog of similar age, fitness level, and breed type. "Things like their walk tolerance is going to be decreased, their ability to get on and off the bed or the sofa," says. Amy Kramer, PT, DPT, CCRT, founder of Beach Animal Rehabilitation Center in Southern California. "They may still try (to do their old activities) because their brain doesn't tell them any differently. That puts them at risk for injury."

▸ Listen Now: Tripawd Talk Radio Episode #71
 The Benefits of Rehab Therapy for Tripawds

Money is tight for everyone after paying for amputation surgery. Rehab therapy is another time and money commitment you probably don't want at the time. But finding a way to cover the cost can save you money in the long run, because you are doing all you can to prevent your dog from getting injured.

Canine rehab practitioners can help in many ways, including:

▶ Locating existing skeletal and muscular weaknesses to reduce the risk of additional damage.

▶ Diagnosing and treating the source of a physical problem instead of relying solely on pain medication that hides symptoms.

▶ Correcting your Tripawd's gait in order to reduce the physical stress of the "Tripawd Hop."

▶ Preventing trauma by strengthening core abdominal muscles required for balance and stamina.

▶ Helping you gain confidence as you watch your Tripawd get stronger.

▶ Entertaining and challenging your dog, physically and mentally.

▶ Improving the overall quality of life for both of you.

Please don't wait to see a therapist. We have been told that most therapists like to see new Tripawds within ten days of amputation surgery. Book at the time of surgery, since most therapy centers have long lead times to get in. Establish a relationship with a great therapist as soon as you know your dog is losing a leg. That way, when (not if) your Tripawd needs pain management and conditioning help in the future, you'll already have a track record with an expert who can help your pup feel better.

You'll be surprised at the fun you can have when you help your Tripawd get strong. Some activities that you might learn how to do together include:

▸ Different types of walking exercises on different surfaces to stimulate the brain and help achieve good balance and foot placement to avoid stumbles
▸ Flexibility and massage movements to stay limber and prevent injury
▸ Weight shifting to promote good balance
▸ Endurance-building activity, like swimming
▸ Land or water treadmill to help your dog learn a better way of walking on three legs.

Your rehab therapist will encourage you to start with small, achievable goals that don't push your pet too hard. A Tripawd who wasn't exceptionally fit before surgery needs more time to build stamina and complete more exercise repetitions. With patience, time, and sticking to homework assignments, your dog can get there!

## How to Find a Qualified Rehabilitation Practice

Veterinary clinics are adding rehabilitation therapy to their menu of services, but just because a practice has an indoor water treadmill doesn't automatically make it a great place for care. To ensure that your dog gets safe, effective rehab, follow these suggestions to find a qualified practice.

When it comes to the best types of animal rehab clinics, these practices feature many of the same following features you expect in your own human medical practice.

### Team members with excellent credentials.

As of today those credentials are good around the world. Look for staff with the initials CCRT, CCRP, CERP, and VMRT after their name. This indicates the therapist has received the best and newest training in veterinary rehabilitation training. If you find a veterinarian who is also a "DACVSMR" (Diplomate of the American College of Veterinary Sports Medicine and

Rehabilitation), this means they have received board certification in sports medicine and rehabilitation.

In the UK, practitioners with the designations of ACPAT, NAVP, and IRVAP also have veterinary physiotherapy training. Canadian practitioners will have "Dipl. Canine Rehab" after their name indicating they are a diplomate of that veterinary rehabilitation specialty.

All good canine rehab therapy centers also have an on-site veterinarian with rehabilitation therapy credentials. A close second would be a veterinarian who oversees the therapy center but isn't necessarily on-site.

## Multiple rehabilitation treatment options.

The ideal clinic offers more than a water treadmill and cold laser therapy. Your dog should have access to as many ways to treat pain and strengthen as possible. Treatments like acupuncture, manual stretching, massage, and newer modalities like shockwave therapy are all good things to work for.

## And a team who is responsive to your situation.

A responsive team means more than friendly staff who returns your calls quickly. You want a team who answers your questions, and gets to know you and your dog on many different levels. Great therapy teams want your dog to heal, and only need to check in occasionally. That's because the goal of canine rehab therapy is not to "hook you in" to ongoing treatments. Good therapy teams understand that money is an issue for 99% of clients. So as long you do your part by communicating your financial ability to treat your dog, and they know your goals and your budget for rehab, that team will be willing to work with you to create a treatment plan with "homework assignments" that put your dog on the path to fewer visits over time.

## Why Choose a Therapy Center with an On-Site Veterinarian?

An on-site veterinarian is important, even if you rarely work directly with that person. See, although non DVM canine rehabilitation practitioners can practice most therapy modalities, someone who is not a veterinarian just doesn't have the level of clinical training that a veterinarian has achieved. Only a veterinarian has the variety of diagnostic tools and experience that can pinpoint pain or possibly notice another condition not at all related to pain.

When a rehabilitation practice doesn't partner with a veterinarian, the entire picture of your dog's health is tougher to see. That lack of comprehensive knowledge about their health puts them at risk of treatments that do more harm than good. For instance, if a Tripawd with cancer suddenly develops back pain, the pet parent might send their dog to the local swim therapy center, which doesn't have a licensed vet on site. After weeks of swim therapy the pain is still there, so the dog goes to their veterinarian who orders x-rays. That's when they discover that cancer has metastasized to the dog's spine. Unfortunately, we've seen this happen in our community. It's hard to say, but if a vet had seen that dog sooner, they could have been experiencing a better quality of life all along, instead of enduring painful and unnecessary swim sessions.

Larger practices with on-site veterinarians usually do cost more money up front. But those practices can actually save you money by helping your dog to feel better sooner. By working with a veterinarian-led team, you get faster access to treatments like pain medication prescriptions, injections, or acupuncture that can only be given by a licensed veterinarian.

## Use These Directories to Find a Qualified Canine Rehab Practice Anywhere in the World

- Vital Vet Find a Rehab Professional Directory
- The Canine Rehabilitation Institute (CCRT) Directory
- North Carolina State University College of Veterinary Medicine Certified Companion Animal Therapist (CCAT) Directory
- University of Tennessee Knoxville Veterinary Academy of Higher Learning (CCRP) Directory
- American Association of Rehab Veterinarians and Vet Techs Global Directory
- Canadian Physiotherapy Association Animal Rehab Division
- United Kingdom Institute of Registered Veterinary & Animal Physiotherapists (VP / MT) Directory
- Australian Canine Rehabilitation Association Directory

## What if You Can't Find a Rehab Therapy Clinic Near You?

If you live in the country far from any big city, you might think that there are no therapy centers within a reasonable driving distance. We have lived in the country ourselves and understand what it's like to live far from services. If that's the case for you, don't panic – there may be a therapist closer than you think. Here's what you can do to try to find the nearest rehab clinic:

**Search the directories listed above.** Expand your search radius to 50 miles or however far you are willing to drive.

**Don't see a therapist listed near you?** Contact the nearest one, and ask if they know anyone nearby or a mobile therapist. It's a small community, and they may know a practitioner who is new or not listed. If they don't know anyone, ask the therapist if they are willing to do a virtual consultation.

**Still can't find a nearby therapy center?** A remote "telehealth" consult with a therapist who isn't nearby may be able to help. Here are some to contact:

- ▶ Upward Dog Rehab & Wellness (Canada-based)
- ▶ The Balanced Dog (Australia-based)
- ▶ Joycare Onsite (US-based)
- ▶ Indy Pet CORE (US-based)
- ▶ Wizard of Paws (US-based)
- ▶ Dogs for Motion Academy (Slovenia, EU-based)

## Here's What a First Tripawd Rehab Therapy Visit Usually Looks Like

The first visit is going to be the most expensive. Remember, Tripawds Foundation can cover the cost of that first therapy visit, so don't panic.

During visit #1, your dog will get a complete exam and evaluation. This visit can take up to two hours. Your dog will receive a full examination by the lead therapist before beginning any therapies. Typically, it looks like this:

- ▶ Your dog's pain level will be evaluated.
- ▶ Gait, stance and body alignment are also examined.
- ▶ The team looks for any neurological disorders
- ▶ They also measure muscle mass and spinal mobility
- ▶ Joint health and range of motion are also assessed.

**!** Get reimbursed for your first rehab visit with a certified therapist from the Maggie Moo Fund for Tripawd Rehab. See https://tripawds.org/rehab

Dr. Ana Esquivel, a practicing veterinarian, rehab therapist, and founder of Ace of Paws canine rehabilitation therapy in Albuquerque New Mexico explains what that visit looks like in Tripawd Talk Radio Episode 117.

The ideal rehabilitation visit will include an assessment and diagnosis. Then they will propose a therapy program consisting of on-site work and homework for you. Usually it's sold as a package deal of a certain number of sessions which are less costly than paying for one appointment at a time.

If you decide to do additional sessions with this clinic, they will provide a clear outline of the therapy goals they envision for your dog. You'll get a detailed outline of how they expect your dog to recover based on their condition and the amount of sessions that you purchase.

## Your Dog's Improved Fitness Is Up to You

Generally, therapists recommend a series of weekly visits to start, then taper off with occasional "tune-ups" throughout the year. With dedicated therapy, a new canine amputee should see results at about three to four weeks after starting treatment at a qualified clinic, according to veterinarians we've interviewed. But this success is really in your hands. Remember, your dog won't do the homework alone, this is a team effort.

If you do your part and faithfully follow the homework assignments provide, somewhere around eight to 12 weeks your dog's condition will usually plateau. That's when the clinic visits usually end, and you can continue your dog's workouts a few days a week at home. Reaching that optimum level of fitness is totally up to you. It's based on faithfully taking your dog to rehab therapy as recommended, and doing your part to follow the team's direction – while being honest if you haven't had the time to do it.

Remember, the goal is to not have to pay for treatments indefinitely, but only need to go back occasionally during the year.

## Consistency is Key

You can pick the best rehabilitation clinic in the country, but if you don't do the homework, you are wasting your money. "Amputees really need the homework (done)," says Dr. Waldman, "because they really have everything to learn over again. And you're also going to be training them in a way they haven't been trained before. Like how it used to be OK to jump up on the bed before and now it's not."

Allowing your dog to jump off the bed, feeding him anything they want and letting them play for hours at the dog park are all things you might have grown accustomed to doing. But if the rehab vet says to stop these activities, listen to them! Bad habits are hard to break, but do it for the health and safety of your Tripawd. Ultimately, rehab therapists can only do so much. Consistency is the key to your Tripawd's successful rehabilitation and ongoing physical fitness.

### Examples of Therapies Used for Rehabbing Dogs

All dogs have different rehab therapy needs. A therapy tool or manual therapy (using hands) method that reduces pain in one dog may not show any benefit in another. An older Tripawd with cancer will have completely different set of physical therapy needs than an eight month old puppy who lost a leg from a car accident. Different breed types and even dogs with different leg configurations will also require different levels and types of strength training. Perhaps the only thing all Tripawds have in common is that both front and rear leg amputees experience some level of chronic pain from the repetitive motions of the "Tripawd hop."

To help your dog get strong and stay injury free, your therapist will create a program that uses different therapies based on your dog's physical needs. Some are hands-based movements such as massage, stretching or chiropractic care. Some are modalities (using tools) with specific functions to treat pain and injury, such as acupuncture or cold laser therapy. The more types of therapy a center offers, the better. They may not use them all on your dog, but it's good to have a variety available.

Rehab therapists incorporate all of these tools into a tailored program that usually addresses three major areas where Tripawds need help:

- Pain Management
- Massage and Manual Therapies (Soft Tissue Mobilization)
- Building Flexibility

Most Tripawds who go to rehab therapy will enjoy a pain-relieving combination of pain medication, acupuncture, massage and soft tissue mobilization, chiropractic care, and cold laser therapy. Let's take a look at the most common treatments studied and approved by the veterinary community.

## Cold Laser Therapy

Low Level Laser Therapy (LLLT) can help with achy joints, painful muscles, and promote incision healing. A therapist may opt to use a small handheld device that emits a low-level, Class 3 laser. When applied to wound tissues or joints, it can help reduce inflammation and promote healing.

Cold laser therapy is a safe treatment for chronic arthritis, surgical incisions, tendon and ligament injuries, and traumatic injuries. However, it's not always right for every dog, especially those with cancer. There is some debate about whether or not cold laser therapy can promote cancer cell growth activity. "If the diagnosis was some form of cancer, we don't always use laser, just for the fear of that maybe causing increased blood flow to the area and if there is still some cancer, we don't want to help that spread," explains Dr. Kramer.

## Acupuncture

This ancient healing technique is based on tapping into the nervous system to treat ailments in the body. In our Tripawd Talk Radio episode #63 with veterinary acupuncturist Dr. Nell Ostermeier, she explains that "acupuncture has become more mainstream over the past 10 years. Most people are familiar with its use for pain relief, injuries and musculoskeletal issues. However, acupuncture is also used to treat internal organ dysfunction and disease, allergies, and behavioral or emotional issues such as anxiety. So, acupuncture can be used to help treat virtually any health condition or imbalance in the body."

Dr. Ostermeier also explains that "Tripawds in general are excellent candidates because their bodies have learned to function in an abnormal way in order to maintain a normal, happy quality of life. While they may make it look easy, it does cause excess wear and tear on the muscles and joints of the other limbs taking up the slack. Acupuncture is excellent for supporting the remaining limbs while they do the extra work. In addition, there has been research into phantom limb syndrome in people which has been shown to respond to acupuncture. It only makes sense that if people experience phantom limb, so could pets."

## Ultrasound

This tool is used to decrease swelling and loosen tight muscles. Humans have benefited from ultrasound since the 1940s, and animals since the 1970s. It uses a combination of sound waves, heat, and vibration to help promote joint flexibility, break down scar tissues, and reduce inflammation. By doing so, it also lowers pain levels, reduces muscle spasms, and promotes wound healing. This <u>VCA article about ultrasound</u> goes into great detail about what to expect with the treatment.

## Manual therapies

The trained hands of a therapist can promote relief, relaxation, balance, and flexibility. Examples of how therapists use their hands include gentle chiropractic care, massage, gentle stretches, passive range of motion (PROM) movements, and balance games. Many manual therapies are the same ones done to help people, only modified and made much more gentle for animals.

A good practitioner has many hands-on methods to use and should offer to teach some to you as part of your homework assignments. Turn to the Merck article "<u>Manual Therapy in Veterinary Patients</u>," for a more in-depth discussion about benefits, contraindications, and possible side-effects.

## Underwater treadmill

Once the pain of an existing injury is brought under control, and when the amputation incision is healed, swimming in an underwater treadmill is great fun for dogs who love water. Some dogs may even learn to love it with the right therapists. It builds strength, endurance, and better movement. Rewards include being trained to use a better gait, building up strength and growing the endurance to play longer and walk greater distances. But a treadmill should never be the *only* tool used by a practitioner

**!** Underwater treadmill therapy is **not** the same as open water swimming.

In our Tripawd Talk interview with Dr. Amy Kramer, we learn that swimming in a pool or pond is great for healthy animals who just need conditioning. However, the underwater treadmill is better for dogs with injuries that need treatment. Because it can help a new Tripawd learn to walk with less hopping, this tool greatly decreases their risk of muscle strains. It can also help build up some strength, tolerance and endurance to allow them to go on longer walks. These are things than open water swimming cannot do.

## Neuromuscular Electrical Stimulation (NMES or "e-Stim")

Often called 'e-stim', therapists place electrode patches on certain muscles of a dog, then attach the patches to a small electronic device. A series of gentle electrical impulses are transmitted to certain nerves, which causes related muscles to contract. The contractions help retrain muscles to function normally. This modality tool is one way to rebuild strength when muscles aren't being used normally.

## Transcutaneous Electrical Nerve Stimulation (TENS)

A TENS device is similar to an e-Stim. It uses electrodes applied to the body to decrease pain and inflammation. The electrodes emit a low level electrical current which disrupts the normal pain perception pathways. The current provides pain relief for arthritis, muscle atrophy, tendon and muscle strains and other muscle and bone injuries.

When the TENS unit electrodes are strategically placed on the body and properly adjusted, they stimulate nerves and muscles. Some rehabilitation therapists shave the pet's fur so the electrodes can make good contact. Wyatt Ray's rehab team, however, told us as long as we used plenty of electrode contact gel and made sure the electrodes touch skin, we didn't need to shave him.

Our own therapist taught us how to use a TENS machine on Wyatt Ray to help with his pain. Your therapist may suggest a consumer-friendly version to buy for home use. You can use it too!

## Pulsed Electromagnetic Field (PEMF) Therapy

Products like The Assisi Loop apply PEMF therapy to the body, with a device that emits pulsing electromagnetic fields. This modality helps heal wounds, reduce post-surgical pain and swelling, address pain from orthopedic injuries, neurological issues, inflammatory conditions, and degenerative movement disorders. It's a therapy that can be done at home or in the clinic, and it's also built directly into many products such as bed mats, dog jackets and portable loops.

## Shockwave Therapy –
## Extracorporeal Shockwave Therapy (ESWT)

The shockwave modality has been used in people since the 1970s. It's a handheld tool only used by trained therapist that emits fast, high energy soundwaves to encourage healing of arthritis, tendon injuries, bone fractures, and to reduce osteoarthritis pain. Shockwave therapy is loud, and mildly painful, requiring light sedation for the patient's comfort. Treatments are given every two to three weeks, and improvement can usually be seen after just two or three treatments.

## Pulsed Signal Therapy (PST)

Similar to PEMF therapy, this modality also creates electromagnetic signals but with a specific type to heal bone and surrounding tissues. It sends signals in the body to encourage repair of damaged cartilage, relieve joint pain, swelling, and improve overall mobility. One small PST study showed that osteoarthritic dogs who received PST therapy performed better than dogs who did not. It is gentle, non-invasive and requires no sedation.

## Hyperbaric Oxygen Therapy

Also known as HBOT, this is a large oxygen chamber that mixes high concentrations of oxygen (about three times the normal amount) and air pressure to heal wounds, decrease swelling, and aid in tissue repair. A good example of a canine patient who can benefit is one who has amputation incision wound healing problems.

## Recommended Reading

See All Tripawd Rehab Success Stories:
https://tripawds.org/tag/rehab/

Rehab Therapy for Tripawds Leads to Better Quality of Life:
Tripawd Talk Radio Episode #117
*Learn how rehab therapy for Tripawds can lead to a better quality of life, prevent injuries, and keep amputee pets happy and strong.*

How Meg Enjoys a Pain Free Tripawd Life
*Learn how three-legged dog Meg enjoys a pain-free life thanks to physiotherapy, weight control, and a mum who advocates for pain management.*

All About Rehab Therapy for Tripawds
*Learn all about the benefits of rehab therapy for Tripawds, with veterinary rehabilitation therapist Dr. Amy Kramer of Beach Animal Rehabilitation Center.*

Complete List of Rehab Therapies Used in Animal Rehabilitation
*The American Association of Rehabilitation Veterinarians*

❗ Reading lists with links to related articles and videos are available in the Premium E-book. Get $5 Off with coupon code BASIC5 at https://tri.pet/teb2

CHAPTER 6
# Diet and Nutrition

## Healthy weight is especially important for all Tripawds.

Your dog is placing extraordinary demands on their body because of that missing leg. It is vital to keep your pup slimmer than other dogs of the same breed-type. Yes, it's a tough thing to restrict food intake when all you want is to spoil your dog rotten. After all, we humans show our love through food. Unfortunately, showering any pet with extra calories is not the smartest thing to do. For a Tripawd, it's life-limiting.

Even one or two extra pounds can harm any pet, but especially a Tripawd. Three-legged pets give subtle clues that they're overweight, but those clues often go unseen because we think our dog is just weak from losing a leg. Sometimes that's the case, but more often a dog looks weak because they have too much weight on their body.

### Three Signs of an Overweight Tripawd Dog

1. **Does your dog fall or face plant at least once a day, even months after recovery is technically over?** That could mean they're getting the wrong type of activity, maybe they need more balance training, or it could indicate they are carrying too much weight.
2. **Does your dog's remaining leg buckle when they walk?** That could indicate weakness from being generally unfit, carrying too many extra pounds, or a little of both.
3. **Are short walks (less than 5 minutes) a struggle?** Most Tripawds need time to build endurance, and walks should never last more than 20 minutes even for a fit three-legged dog. But when *all* walks are tiring, regardless of weather or duration, could indicate they're having a hard time carrying extra weight.

Most of us don't see how quickly our Tripawd puts on weight, but it happens fast because of their new limits on physical activity. Thankfully it's much easier to help a pet lose weight than to drop the pounds on ourselves. After all, unless your Tripawd is a super smart trick dog who knows how to open the refrigerator, we have total control their food intake.

"The most important decision that pet parents make every day regarding their pet's health is what they feed it," says Dr. Ernie Ward, founder of the Association of Pet Obesity Prevention. "You've got the most powerful tool in your hand: the ability to precisely measure food every day," he explains. Most pet parents are shocked to learn that even exercise is not as important as the amount and type of food put in a pet's bowl each day.

"If you have a Tripawd dog," Dr. Ward says, "You'll need to make sure that you are looking at calories. You have to count calories. People with regular dogs, maybe can get away with not being attentive to those details. But YOU have to be very careful. "If you've got a dog with three legs and you're going 'I can't help him stay at a healthy weight because he can't exercise,' I say 'Wrong!' Because you've got the most powerful tool in your hand and that is the ability to precisely measure food every day," he adds. "So if they're getting overweight it's not because of a lack of exercise – it's because of a lack of attention to calories."

**❗ Did you know? Every pound of fat on your dog is the equivalent of five pounds of fat on a human!**

According to the 2022 State of Pet Obesity Report by the Association for Pet Obesity Prevention, the number of overweight pets in the United States is consistently increasing over the years. Currently 59% of dogs and 61% of cats are classified as overweight or obese.

This continues a worrying trend in that results in sky-high vet bills to treat obesity-related conditions. From arthritis to torn cruciate ligaments to osteoarthritis, overweight dogs are prone to living more painful, shorter, and sicker lives.

▶ Overweight animals live on average two years less than their healthy weight counterparts.
▶ Too much weight places excessive stress on a dog's body's skeletal frame and joints

- Overweight dogs expend more energy when walking and playing, which causes unnecessary fatigue
- Excess weight stresses vital organs such as the liver and kidneys, which leaves dogs less able to fight infection and disease
- Being overweight creates conditions that are ripe for severe and costly injuries, such as cruciate ligament tears.

Even if it appears that your three-legged dog is doing OK with that extra weight, remember that every step puts unnecessary, intense wear and tear on their body. It also costs more money at the vet.

## How to Keep Your Dog's Weight in Check

Over time, an extra five pounds on any dog will cause devastating damage, but this is especially true with a Tripawd. If you are in denial about your dog's weight problem, your innocent fur kid will have a hard time on three legs.

If you suspect your dog is bigger than necessary, you have tons of options to help you take off the pounds and get your dog to an ideal weight, such as:

- **Ask your vet for an exam.** You want to rule out other possible issues that cause weight gain, such as Cushing's Disease.
- Keep your dog slightly under the ideal weight for their breed. Check the <u>Purina Body Condition Score Chart</u> to see the body type that your dog should resemble.
- **Take your dog into the clinic for regular weigh-ins.** Most vet practices are happy to weigh your dog at no charge, and without an appointment.
- **Use a kitchen scale to measure your pet's food.** The size and weight of kibble varies from brand to brand. Using the same dry measuring cup each time you switch to a different kibble will give you imprecise measuring results that gradually pack on the pounds. If you invest in a digital kitchen scale, you will always know exactly how much kibble to feed your pet, even if you switch brands. You'll see that the side of a bag of food always shows the guideline for the amount of grams of kibble a dog at a certain weight should eat. Remember though, that's just a guideline. Your vet can help you determine the exact amount you should be

feeding (typically less than the recommended amount for four-legged dogs of your dog's same activity level, breed, and age).

Rotate store bought pet treats with healthy homemade ones. It's no coincidence that pet food treat sales are growing as fast as the pet obesity crisis. We all love buying our pets something special to eat, but they appreciate our homemade pet treats just as much. Just remember to track how many treats you are feeding, then subtract that general amount from daily meals. Replace high calorie treats like flour-based biscuits with healthy snacks like green beans, celery and fruit. You'll need to test new foods to find your dog's favorite, but most dogs will eventually eat these kinds of human foods. And whatever you do, keep processed foods for humans out of your dog's diet as much as possible.

Even if your Tripawd was already overweight before the surgery, that doesn't mean your pup can't lose weight now. Dogs drop weight a lot faster than humans, probably because they can't open a fridge for a midnight snack! While it's tough to be the food police and cut back on their portions at mealtime, in time your dog will understand the new feeding routine and begging for more food will be a thing of the past.

## How to check your pet's weight without a scale.

▶ **Step 1: Do a Rib Check**
Stand over your pet. Can you feel each rib? If you can count your pet's ribs without putting any pressure on them, your pet's weight is probably just right.

▶ **Step 2: Compare Their Ribs to Your Knuckles**
Still not sure what your pet's rib cage should feel like? Here's how to know. Place one of your hands flat on a table. Run a finger from your other hand over the knuckles on your flat hand. Feel the bones? Your pet's ribs should feel like that.

▶ Next, flip your hand over. Run your other hand's fingers on the fleshy, lumpy part between palm and fingers. If your pet's rib cage feels the same, it's time to cut back on calories.

▶ **Step 3:** Stand Over Your Dog
Stand over your dog or kneel over your cat, and run your

hands along the torso from shoulders to hips. You should feel and see an hourglass shape to their figure. Then, examine the side of your pet's body. Do you see a nice tucked-in tummy behind the rib cage? You should not see a low-hanging, saggy belly.

If you suspect that your pet needs weight loss help, first give your veterinary team a call. Weight gain may be due to an untreated condition. Or, maybe you switched brands of kibble and it's more fattening. Either way, it's always smart to check your Tripawd for other issues before making any radical changes to their diet. Hopefully it's just a matter of feeding less, so if your vet comes back with a recommendation to start a weight loss program, here are some tips to make weight loss a success.

## How to help your Tripawd lose weight

According to veterinary rehab therapist Dr. Amber Callaway-Lewis of Treasure Coast Animal Rehabilitation and Fitness in Vero Beach, Florida, these are the most important things to remember about Tripawd eating and exercise.

### Evaluate your pet's food quantity.

Our society is so used to "fluffy" pets! When we see a normal-sized dog or cat, we might think they're underweight. But in a world where over half of pets have too many pounds, what you are probably seeing is an overweight animal. Most dogs are just over fed. Sure, some bigger, active dogs need more calories to enjoy an active life. But the majority just need enough calories to maintain a healthy weight. Think about how much food your pet receives each day. Ask yourself, "Does your pet really need that quantity of food to be happy and to live a healthy life?"

### Everything that goes into your pet's mouth counts as calories.

Calories count, from dental sticks to carrot sticks, pill wraps to chicken broth. Every bit of liquid or solid edible food that goes in counts toward your pet's daily calorie count. Dr. Amber suggests asking ourselves "Can we decrease the calories per cup, and keep them eating the same quantity of food and be happy, but still get them to lose weight and maintain a proper body condition?"

## Walking more is NOT the answer to weight loss

"If you have a new amputee, they're learning how to move and walk again," says Dr. Callaway-Lewis. "We don't want to do a calorie cut, and extra long walks, on a dog who's just learning how to walk on three legs. Same thing with a senior dog who's arthritic." But if you shouldn't take your Tripawd on longer walks, then what? "Don't just assume 'I can walk them more to lose weight," she advises. "We have to balance their nutritional needs with their energy requirements."

Instead of long walks, try these alternative activity ideas suggested by Dr. Amber:

▶ Get your dog to get up and move to another room a few times daily.

▶ Play hide and seek inside the house.

▶ Use food as exercise! Animals who are brand new to living on three legs can participate. Gather some of your pet's daily treats or food, and put it in interactive brain games. Give them the option to play with their food. Create an obstacle course for feeding time!

▶ Place daily food in multiple small bowls throughout the house. Or, hide it in small boxes and ask your Tripawd to find them. Your goal is to encourage movement while doing it as safely as possible.

▶ Serve food on a big platter. Let your pet work to get the food. Stretch out the time it takes for them to eat a meal.

▶ Make your pet's food time enjoyable and fun. And if you're not seeing weight loss results, ask your vet for help. It takes a village to find the right eating and exercise program for all pets, but especially Tripawd dogs.

### Tripawd Weight Loss Examples

Remember that every dog is different. Yours may take longer to drop the extra pounds, or do it faster. As long as you stick to the program and work with your vet, it will happen. For an added serving of inspawration, check out these awesome Tripawd dogs who lost weight after surgery:

## Meg Gets Meg-a-Skinny!

*Obviously, as a Megastar, I've always taken a pride in my figure, but I know as a Tripawd, it's especially important to stay on the skinny side. So…. it gives me great pleasure to announce that since losing my leg six months ago, I have lost a total of….. (drumroll)…. 4 whole kilos!!! (that's 8.8 lbs, for you American Tripawds).*

## Boomer Reaches His New Normal

*It has been 3 months and 10 days now, hard to believe. Boomer has continued to trim down and we have moved to maintaining his weight now. His energy is almost back to his old normal because yesterday he ran around the yard back and forth between Amber and me many times wagging his tail.*

## Meet Lady, a Tripawd Weight Loss Success Story!

*It is much easier for a dog to lose weight than it is for a human. We made minimal adjustments to her diet, and for the first three weeks there was almost no activity, and she still was able to lose 13 pounds.*

# Supplements for Tripawds

Look online or in any health food store and you'll find "miracle" supplements that can restore youth, ease arthritis or even cure cancer. Be warned; most of those claims are not true. We are bombarded with a bewildering array of human and pet health supplements, most of which lack hard evidence to back up their claims. But there are some good supplements out there that may live up to their promises.

We frequently discuss supplements in our Eating Healthy Forum topic. This is a great place to see what foods and supplements other Tripawds members are choosing for their dogs and cats.

Members often ask:
- What supplements should I give, and when?
- What's safe to give a dog during chemotherapy?
- Which supplements should be avoided completely?
- How do I know I'm getting my money's worth?

As you'll see in conversations among members, there's no one "best supplement" for certain diseases, amputee dogs or a pup fighting cancer. What works for one dog may not work for another. Some supplements can be a waste of money. They might not deliver what the manufacturer promises, or the amount necessary to be effective is far greater than your dog would willingly tolerate. There are supplements that can even interfere with surgery or chemotherapy drugs. And what's even scarier is that many supplements can be toxic to animals.

Supplements can be powerful tools to live healthy, but use your good judgement when purchasing them. If something sounds too good to be true, it probably is! This is especially true when it comes to cancer-fighting supplements. The industry is packed with manufacturers who are only out to get your money by making snake-oil claims that their product can prevent or even cure cancer. One of these scam artists even tried to sell in our Discussion Forums! Thankfully he was eventually caught* and sentenced to prison.

> \* COLLEGEVILLE MAN SENTENCED TO 97 MONTHS IN PRISON
> FOR SCHEME TO SELL FRAUDULENT CANINE CANCER DRUGS
> TO PET OWNERS
> US DEPARTMENT OF JUSTICE PRESS RELEASE, FEBRUARY 2024

Many of us have experienced our own success stories with cancer-fighting supplements like mushroom therapy. But remember that no single herb or combination of supplements has ever been scientifically proven by veterinary researchers to prevent or cure canine cancer. When you find a supplement that seems interesting, please discuss it with your vet before purchasing. It could cause GI upset, do nothing at all, and waste your good money that could go toward more effective treatment.

When looking for a more "natural" approach to joint support supplements, things get tricky. Many supplements just aren't what they appear to be. Laboratory testing by organizations like Consumer Lab often find conclude that:

▶ Less expensive herbs are sometimes intentionally used
  to replace those that are more costly.
▶ Accidental substitution can occur if plants are
  incorrectly identified or if the name is misinterpreted.
▶ Some herb manufacturers purposefully adulterate their
  products with drugs presumably to increase their efficacy.

To ensure you are getting your money's worth, we suggest using the "ACCLAIM System" that <u>Dr. Nancy Kay</u> recommends.

## The ACCLAIM Method for Choosing Supplements

**A** A name you recognize. Choose an established company that provides educational materials for veterinarians and other consumers. Is it a company that is well established?

**C** Clinical experience. Companies that support clinical research and have their products used in clinical trials that are published in peer-reviewed journals to which veterinarians have access are more likely to have a quality product.

**C** Contents. All ingredients should be clearly indicated on the product label.

**L** Label claims. Tread carefully when a manufacturer makes label claims that sound too good to be true. Look for realistic label claims that don't make promises, such as "may help with ..."

**A** Administration recommendations. Dosing instructions should be accurate and easy to follow. It should be easy to calculate the amount of active ingredient administered per dose per day.

**I** Identification of lot. A lot identification number indicates that a surveillance system exists to ensure product quality.

**M** Manufacturer information. Basic company information should be clearly stated on the label including a website (that is up and running) or some other means of contacting customer support.

This section will point you to supplement recommendations from veterinary experts to help you make smart decisions about which ones to try. For the purposes of staying within the scope of this book, we will only focus on joint support, arthritis and pain relief supplements. When researching cancer supplements we recommend The Dog Cancer Survival Guide.

## Arthritis Supplements: Are They Necessary?

Arthritis in Tripawds takes a toll. Even the most fit amputee dogs and cats will feel the effects of arthritis. Their altered gait and way of moving puts more stress on the body, which ramps up arthritis effects in Tripawds faster than in a four-legged animal. We encourage you to watch this 30 minute presentation by Dr. Felix Duerr, from Colorado State University's Veterinary Teaching Hospital's Orthopedic Medicine and Mobility Team. We are huge fans of Dr. Duerr, because many years ago, a Tripawd named Alice inspired him to focus his research on arthritis in Tripawds and quadpawds. She had arthritis in most of her joints, and it touched him greatly. "She changed the trajectory of my professional career and inspired me to search for solutions, even if the problems seems insurmountable. Arthritis definitely falls into this category," he says.

In our series of CSU Orthopedic Videos Dr. Felix Duerr explains:
▶ Why arthritis is a major problem in people, dogs, and other animals.
▶ What is the caregiver placebo effect?
▶ What arthritis in dogs looks like and how you can treat it.

It's incredible how similarly arthritis behaves in people and dogs! But we humans are far better at verbalizing our pain, and seeing a doctor sooner. Our pets don't have that luxury, it's just not in their nature to verbalize chronic pain and they don't have the ability to call for a veterinary exam. "Dogs get euthanized more often because of mobility concerns, than cancer," Duerr explains.

## What Joint Supplements are Best?

One of the most common questions asked in the Tripawds Eating Healthy Discussion Forum is; "What joint supplements for Tripawd dogs should I get?" This is an important conversation for you and your vet, since your dog is a unique being with unique needs. Of course there are some supplements that most veterinarians feel comfortable recommending, so let's take a look some popular vet-approved joint supplements for Tripawds.

Let's start with joint health products recommended to one member by our long-time Fairy Vet Mother, Dr. Pam, a Tripawd mom and very experienced in health care for amputee dogs.

## Senior Dog Daisy Starts Slowing Down: Now What?

Read Daisy's story in the Ask the Vet Forum discussion titled, <u>Post-Amputation 3 months in she seems to be slowing down quickly</u>.

It's hard to pinpoint what exactly is happening in the body of any dog or cat, since most of us aren't vets and we don't have all the facts, like lab results. As it turns out, Daisy actually had a urinary tract infection, which wasn't pain-related at all! But in the meantime, we did learn about these vet-recommended joint health supplements that you might want to discuss with your vet. Here's a deeper look at three supplements for older three-legged dogs that can help restore mobility

## YuMOVE

YuMOVE Joint Care PLUS supplement is ideal for canine athletes or stiffer, older dogs who need extra support. These tasty, chewable tablets are packed with Glucosamine and Hyaluronic Acid. They also contain 20% more ActivEase® Green Lipped Mussel (a source of Chondroitin) than their standard YuMOVE products for active dogs.

- Contains 20% more ActivEase® Green Lipped Mussel than our standard formula to help ease joint stiffness.
- Supports joint structure. Glucosamine and N-Acetyl-D-Glucosamine provide basic building blocks of cartilage – the tough connective tissue that protects the joint.
- Helps support mobility. Hyaluronic Acid helps to lubricate and cushion the joint while antioxidants Vitamins C & E

  neutralize free radicals, helping to maintain joint mobility.

## Flexadin Advanced

Flexadin Advanced with UCII supports healthy joints and flexibility in dogs and cats. The company says that based on one study, "UCII has been clinically proven to be more effective than glucosamine and chondroitin.*"

- Enhances a pet's normal repair of cartilage and joints
- Maintains joint function

▶ Promotes joint mobility and flexibility
▶ Works differently than other supplements containing hydrolyzed collagen peptides, glucosamine, chondroitin, or CBD.

## Adequan Canine

As we mentioned in Chapter 4, Pain Management, the medication Adequan Canine has been around for about a decade. It's the only FDA-approved cartilage-protecting treatment that helps dogs get better by treating the disease, not just its symptoms.

▶ Proven to restore joint lubrication, relieve inflammation, and renew the building blocks of healthy cartilage.
▶ Prescribing Adequan Canine early, before cartilage wears away completely, can help improve patient outcomes. Even if arthritis is not diagnosed early, it may help reduce the dog's pain, allowing for increased activity levels.
▶ Available by prescription only.

## Saint Bernard Ophelia is thriving with these vet-recommended supplements.

Meet Ophelia, a Giant Breed Saint Bernard. Her veterinarian created a joint health treatment plan that can giver her every chance at a great quality of life. Ophelia's nutrition regimen included the following supplements.

### CanEVA™

This is an interesting joint support for Tripawd dogs. The base of the joint health product is elk antler. According to CanEVA, the antlers are "harvested during the 'velvet' stage of growth, when the antler contains the most nutritional value found in the inner cartilaginous matrix. Antler is the world's fastest growing mammalian tissue. A mature bull can grow up to 50lbs of antler in 90 days!"

Other ingredients include:
▶ Glucosamine – A building block needed for the body to repair and make cartilage
▶ Chondroitin – A protein that promotes joint cartilage growth and repair

- Collagen – The main support of skin, tendon, bone, cartilage and connective tissue
- Hyaluronic Acid – Nature's Lubricant for skin, joints and eyes
- Omegas 3 and 6 – For energy and cell repair
- Calcium, Magnesium – To maintain strong bones and teeth
- IGF, EGF, Amino Acids – To build muscle mass and strength

### Myos Muscle Formula

We first heard about Myos when it was recommended by rock star vets Drs. Sherman and Deborah Canapp in our "Guide to Pet Prosthetics for Vets and Parents" interview. Myos, as we understand it, is a form of concentrated egg yolk. According to the company, "MYOS uses a single, all-natural ingredient called Fortetropin®. No additives or artificial ingredients. Fortetropin® has been shown in multiple clinical studies to accelerate gains in muscle mass, improve mobility and enhance recovery from injury."

### Cosequin DS

This joint health supplement is a Tripawd joint health supplement recommended by veterinarians for many years. Made by Nutramax, it has a lot of good science behind it. According to the company, the proprietary formula has FCHG49® Glucosamine Hydrochloride and TRH122® Sodium Chondroitin Sulfate.

### HyaflexTM Pro®

This is an interesting joint support recommendation for Tripawd dogs. Ingredients include "a combination of Hyaluronic Acid (HA) N Acetyl Glucosamine (NAG), Methylsulfonylmethane (MSM)." We are familiar with Hyaluronic Acid, because Tripawds Spokesdog Wyatt Ray was taking it after his vet suggested this joint health supplement. See our post, "Ease Osteoarthritis Pain with Hyaluronic Acid Pet Supplements."

## Nellie's New Supplement: Jope, with UC-II®

A new joint health supplement for our Tripawds Spokesdog Nellie caught our attention in 2023. It's called Jope, and was developed by a veterinarian who wanted to help minimize osteoarthritis effects on her own dog, Jope uses UCII (undenatured collagen) as the basis for its formula. Undenatured Collagen is known by the brand name UCII, made in the U.S. by InterHealth USA and licensed to various supplements resellers. It is a food-based product consisting of undenatured type II collagen that comes from chicken sternum cartilage.

There are many types of collagen in our bodies. You may be familiar with collagen that helps build strong nails and beautiful hair, but this kind can help build stronger joints. Most clinical studies about UC-II® have been performed on humans. They conclude that it can build strong, healthy joints and give pain relief for people with rheumatoid and osteoarthritis (OA). These studies have given the FDA enough confidence to determine that UC-II supplements are "Generally Recognized as Safe (GRAS)."

▶ Listen Now: Tripawd Talk Radio Episode #125
Osteoarthritis in Tripawds and How UC-II Helps

When it comes to animals, peer-reviewed studies on dogs and horses have shown equally promising results. It has been used in the equine community for a number of years and recently caught on in the small animal world. Better results can be achieved when UC-II® is given in conjunction with a high quality Omega-3 essential fatty acid oil supplement. That's why Jope has 98 mg EPA & DHA per chew.

Finally, in both dogs and humans, UC-II® has excellent bio-availability, meaning the body does a great job absorbing and making use of in a dose as small as 40 milligrams per day. We think it's worth a shot to see if it eases your Tripawd's osteoarthritis symptoms.

! Try Jope with These Coupon Codes. Your purchase helps support the Tripawds community. Thank you!

Up to 4 Bags, Code: **Partner24!<4**
https://tri.pet/jope-4

Save More on 4+ Bags with Code: **Partner24!>=4**
https://tri.pet/jope-6

## There is No One-Size-Fits-All Remedy

These supplements are a good starting point for a conversation with your veterinarian. Canine rehabilitation therapy experts often know lots about canine joint health supplements and can also recommend the best ones for your Tripawd.

Any supplement always better when combined with other important health practices like taking your dog to a rehab therapist evaluation, maintaining a slimmer than normal weight, and getting regular exams. Get more tips about food and nutrition in the <u>Tripawds Eating Healthy Discussion Forum</u>.

## Recommended Reading

<u>Get Pet Weight Loss Ideas on Tripawd Talk Radio</u>
- Interview with Dr. Ernie Ward, founder of the Association of Pet Obesity Prevention

<u>Trouble's Reducing Diet</u>
- Tripawds Member Shares Successful Diet Plan

**!** Reading lists with links to related articles and videos are available in the Premium E-book. Get $5 Off with coupon code BASIC5 at https://tri.pet/teb2

CHAPTER 7
# Growing Older on Three Legs

Dog's lives are too short. We treasure our time together, inwardly knowing that we will probably outlive our dogs. And we put that thought aside for as long as possible. Then one day, we notice subtle signs of white whiskers on our dog's face. It comes as a surprise even though we knew in our hearts it was just around the corner.

We all want our three-legged heroes to live a long, healthy life. But even the healthiest dog will eventually experience the effects of aging, and more often than anyone expects, cancer. It often happens to the best, even dogs who are the perfect image of canine health. Take Bart, for example.

## Case Study: Bart Faces Old Age After Beating the Odds

When a Tripawd is battling cancer, parents must walk a fine line between living each day to the fullest, while hoping for the best by protecting their Tripawd from repeated exposure to activities that can stress the body. Bart and Darcy were one Tripawd pack who did an exceptional job at learning how to balance the needs of his long-term health while making the most of his athletic gifts.

He was an award-winning gun dog and osteosarcoma survivor. Diagnosed when he was just three years old, Bart is proof that even the most grim prognosis can be turned on its head. In October 2008, only three weeks after completing chemotherapy, this rock-solid hunting dog earned his AKC Senior Hunter Title. In April, 2009 he earned his AKC Master Hunter Title – the highest title an AKC dog can receive. Bart continued competing and winning against four-legged dogs in field trials right up to his retirement. Bart defied the odds and showed outdoor enthusiasts that the loss of a leg did not slow down a champion like him.

This energetic Vizsla learned to enjoy duck work in water, performing therapy work with Wounded Warriors veterans and earned accolades from organizations such as the Vizsla Club of America and the American College of Veterinary Internal

Medicine Foundation. He even won the American Kennel Club's 2013 ACE Award for Exemplary Companion Dog! Bart got his angel wings at age 8 after five years of living life to the fullest, strong and without injury.

## What Does Activity Look Like for a Senior Tripawd?

If your senior dog lost a leg to a terminal cancer like osteosarcoma, you might be tempted to allow your dog to play as long and as much as he wants. That's what we did for our Jerry, figuring he didn't have long to live. But before you do what we did, stop! It pays to approach your three-legged journey with the expectation that your dog will live to a ripe old age. We see it happen all the time in our community, and it doesn't matter if they beat cancer with chemotherapy, immunotherapy, or no follow-up treatment at all. Our Jerry made it two years after his amputation caused by osteosarcoma. Never in a million years did we think he would beat the odds! And in his early days of living on three legs, we let him do too much, too soon. We are writing this book, and continue the Tripawds community, so that no pet parent makes the same mistakes we did, especially when it comes to activity.

Whether you have a front or rear leg amputee, a dog with cancer or without, the long-term physical effects of amputation are predictable. No animal, no matter their size, is immune to the problems caused by an altered gait – even if they wear a prosthetic most of the time, according to orthopedic vets and rehab therapists we have interviewed. The longer a dog lives with three legs, the more pain they will experience if they are left to their own devices and their activity isn't well-managed.

One of our best teachers on this subject is Sasha A. Foster, MSPT, CCRT from the Small Animal Orthopedic Medicine and Mobility team at Colorado State University. According to Foster, the most common issues older Tripawds will encounter are muscle tightness caused by changes in how their spine and gait move.

- Front-leg amputees bear more weight and put more stress on the remaining front limb.
- Rear-leg amputees must keep their remaining leg under their body to move.
- And both types of Tripawds live with abnormal spinal rotation that allows them to move.

The end result for all Tripawds is muscle soreness, tightness, and arthritis of the joints and spine. Expect these issues to impact your dog's mobility because it's not a matter of if a dog will develop an injury, but *when* – especially for senior Tripawds. Thankfully there is so much you can do to minimize the impact on senior dogs.

Foster says we can do a lot to help our aging Tripawd live without pain, such as:

▶ Check in at least twice yearly with your Tripawd's rehabilitation therapist.

▶ Keep your Tripawd slim. Any extra pounds put your pet at risk of injury.

▶ Give your Tripawd consistent, safe, vet-approved endurance exercise. Swimming, underwater treadmill and shorter, more frequent walks of 10-15 minutes are great.

"Keep them in the right weight that they're supposed to be for their breed," says Foster. "Make sure they get endurance exercise every day. Great endurance exercises for Tripawds are things like just going for a walk, going swimming is a great thing, doing underwater treadmill if there is a treadmill near you, things to keep their endurance level up so they just have a higher level of fitness."

Checking in with a rehab therapist even more than you would with your regular vet, who typically only recommends doing an exam every six months for senior Tripawds. "We can find things in those evaluations that the animals would not tell us exist," says Foster. "Like tight muscles or sore joints. Then we can treat those things before they become actual injuries."

An older Tripawd is going to be trickier to troubleshoot when they are suffering from pain. Most senior dogs already have some degree of osteoarthritis and unusual gait caused by mobility problems. You can catch changes earlier if you take regular videos of your Tripawd at least once a month. That way you can compare how they move when you suspect an issue, against how they moved before the suspected problem. And don't wait to see your therapist if you suspect your Tripawd is injured. The "wait-and-see" approach is never a good idea. "If you have a Tripawd animal, we would recommend not waiting because the dog or the cat may have an injury that would prevent them from moving. And that injury needs to be addressed sooner than later because they only have the one leg to stand on," says Foster.

## Meg: A Role Model on Three Legs

Meg from the UK is another great example of what life can look like when you aren't dealing with a cancer diagnosis. She was not an exceptionally athletic or active dog, but she had an excellent quality of life because of her mom's dedication to ongoing physiotherapy check-ins and faithfully following the exercises prescribed by Meg's therapist. Clare gave Meg a fantastic life as a Tripawd, until she passed at a ripe old age.

### It wasn't cancer that took her leg.

Meg was from the UK, and born with malformed bones in her front legs. When she was just three, one elbow fractured. After several unsuccessful repairs to the elbow, followed by a serious infection from metal implants in the leg, Clare was faced with the decision to amputate the damaged right leg. She had to hope that her front left leg could withstand the extra load over a lifetime, and the decision wasn't made lightly. "It was nine months of trying to save her leg, during which she'd spent more than two months as an inpatient in hospital," says Clare in this Tripawd Talk interview. "She wasn't in a good way. And frankly, I was I wasn't in a good way either."

But after meeting London veterinary surgeon and physiotherapist Philippa Mitchell of Active Pet Veterinary Rehabilitation, Acupuncture, and Hydrotherapy, Clare found hope for Meg's future. "I didn't even know that people like Philippa existed!" she told us. After Philippa applied many laser treatments and other therapies to try to save the leg, it was clear that amputation was Meg's only option for a good quality of life. "The concern was there wasn't a lot of bone left around those metal implants which were holding Meg's elbow together," recalls Philippa. "And if we didn't do something, then chances were it was going to fracture. Meg would be in quite a lot of discomfort if that happened, and it would be more of an emergency procedure."

### Physiotherapy made all the difference

Within a week of her amputation, Meg returned to Philippa for ongoing rehabilitation therapy. "We'd ideally like to see them about three days after (amputation). For most cases, that's fairly safe for getting them in and out of the car and things like that. Then we can be looking at the wound and making sure everything's healing. We can start doing some laser on it, getting our owners to do exercises and things to help them."

Over time, Meg's pain levels were brought under control, and she began to really enjoy seeing Philippa's team. Once her initial amputation recovery treatments were done, and Clare was confidently doing her home exercises, Meg saw Philippa for periodic check-in treatments that included things like acupuncture, laser therapy, ketamine injections, homework assignments with brain games and other mentally stimulating activities, and the <u>osteoarthritis monoclonal antibody therapy</u> known in the US as Librela.

After our interview, Meg went on to live to a ripe-old age of 13. Her quality of life exceeded that of many four legged dogs. Having a long-term relationship with Philippa was indispensable for Meg's comfort and happiness. Before Meg's passing, Clare told us in the interview that "One thing that I really value is having that regular contact with somebody who knows her body so well," says Clare. "If I go and see Philippa every month, then she's got a really good standard to measure against every month," says Clare. "I think that's been absolutely invaluable. I mean, both for Meg but also for my peace of mind."

## What Can You Do with a Senior Tripawd?

Keeping an older Tripawd entertained with something other than walks is critical for their quality of life. A senior dog is just like a senior human; when they start slowing down physically, the brain is right behind and without any extra stimulation, <u>Canine Cognitive Dysfunction</u> takes over. That's when a dog shows signs of dementia, similar to behaviors also often seen in older people.

### Cognitive Dysfunction Syndrome Overview

Many Tripawds members bring up "<u>cognitive dysfunction</u>" in our Discussion Forums, so it's not an uncommon condition whether a dog has three legs or four. One of the best ways that you can minimize the impact is to introduce interactive brain games to your dog, if you didn't do it during their amputation recovery phase. Other activities we love include the following.

## Teach Your Dog to Paint!

We can't think of a better way to engage your dog's brain than creating beautiful works of art. Every dog has this ability! Download our four-session instructional video course now and learn how to teach your dog to paint.

Get the best dog painting tips from certified trick dog trainer Natasha Baguley. Your workbook includes private links to four tutorial video sessions and a complete supplies list with all of the materials you will need to get started.

**!** Download the Teach Your Dog to Paint video course and workbook at https://tri.pet/dogpaint
Proceeds support the Kaiserin Cancer Care Fund.

## Scent Work Keeps Tripawds Healthy and Hoppy

Scent work for Tripawds keeps pets engaged and entertained. You don't need a ton of equipment, and it's something you can do at home on your own or out with a club. Tune into Tripawd Talk Radio episode #109 for a chat with The Brainy Canine who tells us about how to get started.

## Senior Tripawds Can Live Exceptional Lives on Three Legs

Search through our Tripawds Size and Age Matters Discussion Forum, and you can see that caring for an older Tripawd doesn't have to mean a boring, bubble-wrapped life. Our community has enjoyed the company of hundreds of amazing, super senior Tripawd dogs we've met over the years. Most are family dogs, who just love being with their people and aren't active in any kind of sports. All of these wonderful examples show us that with a careful balance of pain management, a slim body weight, safe and monitored activity, and a skilled vet team, it is possible for a dog of any age or size to live a rich, full life.

You don't need tons of money to give that to them either. Follow our Tripawds News blog for fitness tips. Stay in touch with the community and ask tons of questions. Establish a relationship with a quality veterinary rehabilitation team. And faithfully check in at least a couple of times a year with your rehab therapist. Your Tripawd's quality of life depends on it.

## Your Tripawd's Life is Already Better!

By reading this book you have taken the first step to improve your dog's chance at a healthy, strong life on three legs. That is way more than we were able do do when Tripawds founder Jerry lost his leg to cancer. We didn't know about rehab therapy in 2006, and nobody thought he would live another two glorious years. Had we known, we would have learned more about avoiding long-term joint damage and physical stress to his body.

All we wanted was for him to be a dog, and we made a ton of mistakes doing that. Thankfully, in the end, he lived his life to the fullest despite the cancer. Later, when our second Tripawds Spokesdog Wyatt was living his life, we learned how to avoid making those same blunders with him. And now with our third Tripawds Spokesdog Nellie, we are able to put it all together to ensure that her malformed leg does not lower her quality of life.

Plenty of of veterinarians and rehabilitation therapist professionals know much more about everything that can be done to help our dogs lead a strong, injury free life on three legs. Please work with them! We hope that your Tripawd will also benefit from this knowledge, and the experiences of the generous members who help make Tripawds the number one resource and support community for animal amputees.

! <u>Visit our Hopping Around Discussion Forum</u> for more ideas and to share your own experience.

! <u>Subscribe to Tripawds News!</u> Catch the latest canine rehab therapy information that we are learning and passing along to members like you.

! <u>Get free rehab for your Tripawd</u> with reimbursement for your first consultation with a certified canine rehabilitation therapist.

Thank you for reading. We hope you find this information useful and visit the many resources provided for more information. Now, your Tripawd's fitness is up to you, the best advocate for your amazing amputee who wants nothing more than to have tons of quality time living their best life on three legs. Together, we can show the world that "It's better to hop on three than to limp on four!"

– RENE AGREDANO AND JIM NELSON
FOUNDERS, TRIPAWDS.COM

## Save on Premium E-books

Thank you for downloading this Basics version of our Tripawds recovery and care handbook. For more comprehensive information, numerous photographs, additional resources, and bonus material, download the Three Legs and a Spare Premium E-book.

❗ Get $5 OFF Premium Three Legs and a Spare E-book with Coupon Code BASIC5 at https://tri.pet/teb1

Be sure to check out Loving Life on Three Legs, the Premium Edition. This expanded interactive PDF includes numerous direct links to videos, podcast interviews and more to help you keep your dog healthy and strong after amputation recovery.

❗ Get $5 OFF Premium Loving Life on Three Legs E-book with Code BASIC5 at https://tri.pet/teb2

Get two premium e-books in one! Download the Tripawds Library to save on both Three Legs and a Spare and Loving Life on Three Legs.

❗ Get $10 OFF the Tripawds E-book Library with Code BASIC10 at https://tri.pet/teblib

# Acknowledgements

Loving Life on Three Legs is the second e-book based on informative content compiled from years of interviews with veterinary professionals and the shared experiences, tips and suggestions of pet parents from around the world who participate in the Tripawds global community.

Like the Tripawds community website, this book is intended to be an interactive research tool. The ideas we share represent the personal experiences of members who have learned how to make the most of life on three legs in a variety of circumstances. None of the information contained on Tripawds or found within these pages is meant to replace one-on-one medical care from your regular veterinary team.

We dedicate this book to every Tripawds member, including YOU! From submitting guest blog posts to Tripawds Foundation donations, to taking time from your busy day to participate in the forums, Tripawds would not be able to help others through their own three-legged journey without the inspirational stories of people like yourself.

A very special shout out goes to Maggie the Agile Cow Dog and her mom Tracy. This dynamic duo were the first members who enlightened us about the benefits of canine rehabilitation therapy. Maggie lived to over age 13 and now, because of their participation in the Tripawds community, we are all learning how to help our amputee dogs live healthy, fit and safe lives on three legs.

We also want to express our sincere gratitude to every veterinary professional who has kindly helped us share accurate and current information to the Tripawds community. Thank you from the bottom of our hearts. Without your participation and generous support, Tripawds would not be the vet-approved resource that it has become.

With gratitude,

**René Agredano, Jim Nelson, and Nellie B. Dawg**

Dedicated to Angel Wyatt Ray Dawg and Spirit Jerry G. Dawg

# Appendix

## About the Tripawds Community

Tripawds is the world's largest online support community for amputee pets and their people. Made possible by the Tripawds Foundation, a 501c3 public charity, our community hosts 1500+ three-legged dog and cat blogs, popular discussion forums, a 24/7 live chat room, video interviews and photo galleries, and the Tripawd Talk Radio podcast. The foundation hosts the toll-free Tripawds Helpline and offers various direct assistance programs for pet parents facing amputation for their beloved pets. Start here for an overview of the many Tripawds resources.

### Who is Jerry, and How Did Tripawds Begin?

http://tri.pet/jerrygdawg

Jerry was the first Chief Fun Officer of our home-based marketing firm, Agreda Communications. In those early days, we enjoyed many hikes together in the mountains of Northern California, and spent numerous evenings playing with him on the beach after he encouraged us to step away from work and enjoy life. After one long weekend hiking, Jerry started limping, and we learned that dogs get cancer. Before we knew it, he had a forelimb amputated because of osteosarcoma, a deadly canine bone cancer.

Tripawds Chief Administrator Jim Nelson coined the term "Tripawds" after hearing vets and techs at U.C. Davis refer to amputee dogs as tripods. He registered the tripawds.com domain to reclaim and empower the term in late 2006.

To enjoy every remaining moment we had left with Jerry, we sold everything we owned and bought an RV to travel the country together as a pack. In 2009, PBS told our story in the documentary, Nature: Why We Love Cats and Dogs. Along the way, Jerry defied the odds and lived two incredible, adventure-filled years, while demonstrating the fine art of living in the Now.

While coping with Jerry's diagnosis, we started a little blog about Jerry, as a way to share our adventures and document his treatment plan and share his progress with friends and family. The blog's readership grew, and soon we began receiving pet amputation and limb cancer questions from people all over the globe.

After being inundated with emails from people with all sorts of questions about canine cancer and amputation, Jim installed discussion forums as a way to help pet parents like us connect with one another, share the stories of their own three-legged dogs and ask each other questions about pet amputation recovery and care. Later, Jim added a live chat room and then built the Tripawds Blogs network to host free three-legged dog and cat blogs for members.

We continue or nomadic lifestyle today, managing the community from our mobile Tripawds headquarters. In 2019, we published our book which tells the full story – ***Be More Dog: Learning to Live in the Now***.

In 2014, we created the Tripawds Foundation, a 501c3 charity to ensure that these many resources remain free and available to those in need. The Tripawds Foundation serves as an educational and support forum, providing resources for individuals and organizations seeking information related to animal amputation and related health conditions. The foundation now provides various direct financial assistance programs for Tripawd pet parents.

Today, the Tripawds Community is the largest online support community for amputee pets and their people. Our trustworthy information and resources has won the approval of veterinary professionals around the globe, who frequently refer amputation clients to our community for information and emotional support. We consider their endorsement the highest honor, and strive to always maintain that trust.

**! Tripawds Mission Statement:** To maintain a community of support for those faced with amputation for their pets, by providing informational resources and a platform for discussion.

## Tripawds Featured Blogs

Tripawds hosts free three-legged dog and cat blogs for anyone who wishes to share their pet's story or document their chosen treatment plan. Tripawds Supporter Blogs with enhanced features and data storage space are available for a nominal annual fee, the proceeds of which help offset the costs of maintaining our community. The following Tripawds Featured Blogs provide information and resources to educate members about the care and treatment of pet cancer survivors and other amputee animals.

## Tripawds News

https://tripawds.com

Find all articles and many more resources including the popular discussion forums, live chat, photo galleries and videos.

## Tripawds Gear Shop

https://gear.tripawds.com

Learn which products are best for three-legged pets by checking out Tripawds Gear product reviews, exercise tips, and demonstration videos about the three-legged life. Here you will find information about popular, helpful tools like dog harnesses, flotation vests and exercise equipment.

## Tripawds Nutrition

https://nutrition.tripawds.com

Search Tripawds Nutrition blog archives for years of diet and nutrition articles, member-tested treat recipes, and more.

## Tripawds Gifts

https://gifts.tripawds.com

Show your Tripawd Pride with fun three-legged dog amd cat designs on t-shirts, bandannas, custom jewelry, and more.

## Tripawds Downloads

https://downloads.tripawds.com

Find all Tripawds e-books and other helpful downloadable resources in the Tripawds Downloads Store. All Tripawd Talk Radio podcast episodes are also archived in the Downloads blog.

## Tripawds Foundation

https://tripawds.org

Visit the Foundation Blog for information about all our assistance programs, <u>Tripawds Honor Roll</u> tributes, <u>sponsorship opportunities</u>, and grant recipient profiles.

## Tripawds Auctions

https://auction.tripawds.com

Check this site for our annual Tripawds Painting Dogs Auction or download the Teach Your Dog to Paint video course and join the fun next time!

## Be More Dog

https://bemoredog.net

Get our <u>Be More Dog</u> book or find commentary and excerpts with photos and videos from passages in the book.

## Wyatt Ray's Dawg Blog

https://wyattraydawg.tripawds.com

Follow the three-legged adventures of Tripawds Spokespup II, <u>Wyatt Ray Dawg</u>. See his crazy adventures and fun videos from traveling the country with his pack.

## All About Nellie B Dawg

https://wyattraydawg.tripawds.com

Check in on our honorary Tripawds Spokesdawg III to see where Nellie's adventures are taking her now.

## The KillBarney Blog

https://killbarney.tripawds.com

Discover the legacy of the <u>KillBarney tour</u>, see <u>where it went</u>, and learn all about <u>Jerry's love/hate relationship</u> with a certain small, purple, fuzzy dinosaur. Or get the <u>KillBarney Tour Book</u> filled with original journal entries from Tripawds members around the world.

**Subscribe to all blogs at https://tripawds.com/subscribe**

# Free Tripawd Heroes E-book!

**How will your dog cope after amputation? Just ask these Tripawd Heroes!**

Download your free copy of Tripawd Heroes for more than 20 inspirational canine  amputation success stories of dogs  loving life on three legs.

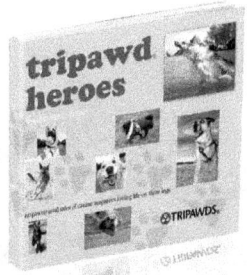

**Plus:** receive our best pet amputation recovery and care tips, and videos of veterinarians answering common questions.

Free Download: https://tripawds.com/heroes

@tripawds

Team #Tripawds with Wyatt Ray at 2018 Western Veterinary Conference

# TRIPAWDS.
## .com

## Tripawds Publications

Three Legs and a Spare

Loving Life on Three Legs

Cool Tips for Tripawd Cats

Be More Dog: Learning to Live in the Now

Tripawd Heroes

The KillBarney Tour

Find All Tripawds E-books at:
https://downloads.tripawds.com

## TRIPAWDS
## FOUNDATION
### A 501C3 PUBLIC CHARITY

## Tripawds Foundation

Find information about assistance programs and
how you can help at:

https://tripawds.org

@tripawds

www.ingramcontent.com/pod-product-compliance
Lightning Source LLC
Chambersburg PA
CBHW050349280326
41933CB00010BA/1399